Tour!

Mini Book Series

VOLUME XXIV

By

Ronald Pattinson

Mini Book Series volume XXIV: Tour!

Copyright © 2015 Ronald Pattinson

The right of Ronald Pattinson to be identified as the author of his work has been asserted by him in accordance with the

COPYRIGHT, DESIGNS AND PATENTS ACT OF 1988

All rights reserved. No part of this publication may be reproduced, stored in a retrieval system, or transmitted, in any form or by any means without the prior written permission of the publisher, nor be otherwise circulated in any form other than that in which it is published and without a similar condition being imposed upon the subsequent purchaser.

1st edition

Published in August 2015 by

Kilderkin
171 hs Warmondstraat, Amsterdam, Noord- Holland

ISBN 978-94-90270-27-8

Mini Book Series volume XXIV: Tour!

Contents

Tour!	1
Foreword	5
I East Coast	6
Boston	7
Boston still	10
New York City	12
Brooklyn	15
Brooklyn (part two)	18
Philadelphia	22
Philadelphia (part two)	24
Philadelphia (part three)	28
Williamsburg	33
Williamsburg (part two)	35
Washington	40
Washington and Baltimore	43
Back in Boston	45
Farewell to Boston	47
II San Diego	50
San Diego	51
Brewing at Stone	52
Brewing at Stone (part two)	57
California day three	61
California day three (part two)	65
California day four	71
California day four (part two)	75
III Mid-West and Canada	79
Toronto day one	80
Toronto day one (part two)	84
Toronto day two	90
Toronto airport	95
Chicago day one (part one)	96
Chicago day one (part two)	99
Chicago day two	104
Grand Rapids day one	106
Grand Rapids day two	108
Grand Rapids day three	112
Grand Rapids day four	115
A few hours in Toronto	118
IV Pacific Northwest	121
Seattle day one	122
Seattle day two	127
Denver day one	132
Denver day two	135
Portland day one	140
Portland day two	144

Mini Book Series volume XXIV: Tour!

    Vancouver day one 149
    Vancouver day two 155
    Seattle day three 160
    Seattle day four 166
V The South 167
    Houston day one 168
    Houston day two 171
    Birmingham day one 176
    Birmingham day two 180
    Atlanta day one 186
    Atlanta day two 194
    Asheville day one 198
    Asheville day two 205
    Asheville day two (part two) 211
    Houston final day 215
    Houston Airport 220
VI California 221
    Take California 222
    California! 224
    California! Amsterdam 227
    Take the Caltrain 231
    The infamous breakfast 234
    The dark side 238
    California Mild 243
    That's my country! 248
    The Haight 253
    Freewheeling in Frisco 260
    A busy day in San Diego 269
    Dossing with Diego 277
    Mexico 285
    Farewell to Sandy Ego 294
    Home 303
Index 304

Mini Book Series volume XXIV: Tour!

Foreword

"You're crazy, Ronald." My wife Dolores told me countless times, as I planned, fretted over and executed six trips to the USA. Pushing my book, "The Home brewer's Guide to Vintage Beer".

She had a point. I bounced around the country like a hyperactive rubber toddler. From bottom left to almost top right. And lots of bits between. (Apologies if I got too geographically technical there.)

This is the story of my travels. Sometimes, beer by beer, frequently more fanciful. An outsider bumbling through a brash and often bemusing, beer culture. Where I encounter brewers, beers, bars and the random characters that hang around them. While bemoaning sludgy beer, praising cask, counting beards and describing my breakfasts in ridiculous detail.

As I tart my book with mixed success. From frankly fantastic down to downright depressing. While still having more fun than should be legal. Meeting old friends, making new ones and, obviously, drinking lots of beer. Mostly pretty good. Bourbon, too. (Probably more than I should, even when mostly medicinal.)

Best bit? Easy. Brewing at Colonial Williamsburg. The most fun I've had without breaking either a sweat or the law. Other memorable moments: hanging on the Haight, Dann dressing up, the infamous breakfast, generosity of strangers, wildfires, radio, snow storms, train rides, greyhounds, steelworks, Canada, vomit. Mashtun hot tub, barbecue, airport chat. And lots of taxi rides.

In these pages you'll live the journeys with me, see them through my eyes. My fat, knackered, old git eyes. When I manage to keep them open.

Ron Pattinson.

Amsterdam, 9th July 2015.

Mini Book Series volume XXIV: Tour!

I East Coast

Mini Book Series volume XXIV: Tour!

Boston

Just as well my plane was on time and the queues at immigration short. Because my first appointment is a mere two hours after my scheduled touchdown.

Arival at Boston runs perfectly smoothly. Unlike departure from Amsterdam. Mistaking my natural sweatiness for anxiety, I get nearly the full security works. It stops just short of getting my grillox out. Dontcha just love air travel?

I have enough time to unpack my undies, log on to the internet and catch my breath a little before Dann and Martha (of Pretty Things) pick me up and whisk me off to the radio studio. Where I'm set to appear on Digradio's Good American programme.

http://thegoodamericancollective.blogspot.com/2014/03/the-good-american-radio-show-feat_8.html

It's my first radio appearance, but, having done plenty of podcasty things and Skype interviews, nothing too daunting. We chat a bit about our latest collaboration: 1955 Whitbread Double Brown. (A beer I keep telling everyone is in my book, The

Mini Book Series volume XXIV: Tour!

Homebrewer's Guide to Vintage Beer, until I realise it was one of the recipes I'd had to cut for space reasons. Whoops. It was a couple of days before I twigged.)

I'm dead pleased when Dann suggests spending the evening in Deep Ellum. I feared I might miss the chance to drop by one of my favourite US bars. Especially as they had the 1955 Double Brown on tap. We cracked a bottle during the radio show, but I only got a couple of mouthfuls.

It's packed. Which I guess is a good sign. It's Friday night, after all. We wait for a table, trying not to get too much in the way of the waiting staff.

My only complaint is the mood lighting. I struggle to read the beer menu. Not that I try much (anything? I can't remember) other than the 1955.

By the end of the evening I'm struggling with fatigue, too. But I manage to prop my eyes open until 23:00 or so. Then off for a well-earned kip. In preparation for a busy day.

Mini Book Series volume XXIV: Tour!

digradio
http://digboston.com/tag/dig-radio/

Deep Ellum
477 Cambridge St,
Boston, MA 02134.
Tel: +1 617-787-2337
http://www.deepellum-boston.com/

Mini Book Series volume XXIV: Tour!

Boston still

Unsurprisingly, given my state of knackeration, I sleep well. But more importantly I wake up. And at the right time.

I've a breakfast appointment with Dann and Martha. They take me to a diner in Somerville for exactly the breakfast I need. The type of egg and bacon combination that will have the cholesterol dancing in my arteries. That and lots of coffee.

I've pretty much abandoned breakfasting in American hotels. It rarely comes included

Mini Book Series volume XXIV: Tour!

and a diner always trumps it for atmosphere, price and often quality, too. I love American diners, and I'm sure it's not just a false nostalgia engendered by film and TV. Like London cafes, they offer a glimpse into daily life and daily lives. And they sell bacon. Gotta lovem.

Bellies full, we drop by the Pretty Things office, also in Somerville. We're picking up the stuff for the evening's 1955 Brown Ale launch at the Independent, located just around the corner. Then move on to the Independent to start setting up. Decorating tables, hanging up banners, that sort of thing.

A love of dressing up is one of Pretty Things' most loveable features. Once again, they don't disappoint. Dann has a particular knack for getting the facial hair spot on. I think you'll agree that this was another triumph.

Makes me wish I had a costume, too.

No idling around listlessly before the evening event. Dann fills the afternoon with an industry do in their office. Where, as a special treat, there's cask Double Brown. Sorry all you craft fan boys, but, once again, here is proof of the superiority of a well-handled cask over keg. It wees all over it. Every day of the week, every month of the year.

Pulled through a sparkler, both the head and carbonation level are spot on. Flavour isn't cask's only trump. There's also its drinkability. A higher temperature and lower carbonation ease its way down your neck almost unnoticed. A few pints quickly evaporate as I chat with old friends and new acquaintances. There will be little time for chatting later on.

The evening in the Independent is busy, loud, slightly anarchic, but loads of fun. Given the crowds, noise and general boisterousness, it's just as well I really do say just a few words. My shortest talk of the tour by at least an hour.

I'm so occupied by signing books and chatting to punters that it's only when I'm back in the hotel that I realise I forgot to try the other Pretty Things beers being launched, Grampus. A double-mash monster of a beer. Then again, given the length of the day, sticking to the modestly-strengthened Double Brown perhaps wasn't such a bad idea.

Having an early start the next day, I don't stay up late. We're all off to New York City for more events, more beer and hopefully lots more ~~beer~~ fun.

The Independent
75 Union Square,
Somerville
Tel: 617 440 6022
http://www.theindo.com/

Mini Book Series volume XXIV: Tour!

New York City

I need to be checked out and ready to roll by 9 AM. Dann and Martha are driving me down to New York and want a reasonably early start.

Originally, I didn't plan travelling to New York until Monday. Then Dann arranged an additional event in New York on the Sunday, at Jimmy's No. 43. Bang went one of my two rest days.

We pick up breakfast on the way down. I dodge breaking my 27-year McDonalds fast by getting something from Boston Market instead. (February 1987 in New Orleans was the last time, in case you're wondering. Don't ask me why I even ate it then. It wasn't my choice.)

We all nod off at some point during the journey. Except for Dann. Just as well, as he's driving. I find a conscious driver infinitely more reassuring than a slumbering one.

First we drop off the beer at Jimmy's, before continuing on to our hotel in Brooklyn. I've not been to Brooklyn for a long while. Since I lived in New York. Almost as long - spring 1987 - as since I last ate McDonalds. I don't feel quite so guilty about easing over the East River as I would about easing down a greasy burger.

We stay in an interesting part of Brooklyn. 90% of the locals are Orthodox Jews and the streets around our hotel are filled with beards, long black coats, odd hats, prams and children. That extends to the hotel itself, except for the kids. My room is clean and tidy. Though the pillar in the middle of it was a bit odd.

I'm excited to drink in Jimmy's. The East Village was one of my preferred piss-up locations during my NYC time. Jimmy's is right in the middle of where I lived out many of my most memorable drinking evenings. Not that I can remember any of them it great detail. It was all a very long time ago.

Jimmy is quite a character, ebullient and garrulous, flitting this way and that to greet and chat, perpetually in motion. And always shaking hands. We must shake a dozen times in the first hour. The perfect character for a publican.

Jimmy keeps beer and appetisers coming. There's also a constant flow of people come to chat with me and Dann, a few books are sold and more are signed. But it's quieter than at the Independent and I've more chance to knock back a few beers. I've a good excuse: I have to grab the chance to drink draught 1955 Double Brown while I can.

It's a lovely beer, but I'd expected nothing less. A Whitbread recipe and Dann's brewing skill were always going to hit the bullseye. It's bitterer than you might expect from and British Brown Ale, but that's backed up by plenty of malt. A great drinking beer. I think we did it justice.

Mini Book Series volume XXIV: Tour!

We don't stay too late. There's still time for a barbecue dinner in a trendy, garage-like space back in Brooklyn (Fette Sau). Though my memories of the meal are almost as blurred as the photos I took.

We'll be meeting Jimmy again tomorrow. When he interviews me and Dann in the middle of hipster Brooklyn.

Jimmy's No. 43
43 E. 7th St.,
New York, NY 10003.

Pointe Plaza Hotel
2 Franklin Ave,
Brooklyn, NY 11249.
Phone: +1 718-782-7000

Mini Book Series volume XXIV: Tour!

Fette Sau
354 Metropolitan Ave,
Brooklyn, New York 11211.
Tel: +1 718-963-3404
http://www.fettesaubbq.com/

Mini Book Series volume XXIV: Tour!

Brooklyn

Monday is the busiest day of the tour so far. Two radio interviews and an event.

Just as well, then, that we rise early again. The hotel includes breakfast, but just a buffet. I want something more bacony. Luckily Dann and Martha agree. Off we head in their van into deepest Brooklyn. Through streets that had seen better days, clad in decayed and sometimes crumbling Victorian grandeur. I love old brownstones. They remind me of the buildings I see in my dreams.

Our destination is Tom's Diner (officially Tom's Restaurant), a renowned breakfast haunt, which, if the photos adorning the place are to be believed, has been frequented by movie stars and popular singers. I go for my usual egg and bacon combination. Can't go wrong with that. Especially when the day ahead is long and busy.

On the wall next to our table are the lyrics of Suzanne Vega's Tom's Diner. Proof that at least one pop singer came here. To be honest, I'm more concerned by the quality of my fry up than which of the famous have eaten here before me. Luckily, it doesn't disappoint. My breakfast, I mean. It's soon safely curled up inside me, sleeping peacefully.

Fed, we need to scuttle quickly across Brooklyn to Roberta's, in a deceptively industrial-looking area of town. It's a pizza place with attached radio studio. I know, weird. But this is Brooklyn. The scavenged construction reminds me of squatted (or formerly squatted) venues in Amsterdam.

As we're still waiting for Jimmy to arrive, I stave off dehydration with a Bell's Two

Mini Book Series volume XXIV: Tour!

Hearted, a beer I've not tried before. It comes in what look like a jam jar. It's made out of glass - what do I care? It's full of than Americany IPA-style flavour. You know what I mean, the grapefruit thing. It's a pleasant enough breakfast beer.

We record three 15-minute segments with Jimmy. Dann and I are joined by John Holl, editor of All About Beer. It's quite a good laugh. Never much chance of the conversation lagging with Jimmy there.

Done and it's time to eat. In Roberta's, obviously, as we're already there. I have a pastrami sandwich. Just because it sounds so New York. It's rather good, but way too much for me. I've forgotten how much meat they stuff into sandwiches over here.

Fascinating for you, me describing my lunch. It came with some crisps, I almost forgot to tell you. I'm sure you needed to know that.

It's time for our next interview, this time with Chris and Mary of Heritage Radio's Fuhmentaboudit! But we don't head back to the studio. That's been booked by someone else. We're off to Brouwerij Lane where we'll be interviewed using a little portable

Mini Book Series volume XXIV: Tour!

recorder.

It's still a little chilly in Brouwerij Lane, but there's beer to drink and the wood-burning stove at the back is gradually chewing away at the cold. Chris and Mary are remarkably professional. They've clearly been at this radio thing for a while. Just two 15-minute chunks this time. They're done in a flash.

The main event is still to come. My book event in Brouwerij Lane. But before that Dann, Martha and I will eat a Polish meal. Try to contain your excitement.

Tom's Restaurant
782 Washington Ave,
Brooklyn, NY 11238.
Phone: +1 718-636-9738

Roberta's
261 Moore St,
Brooklyn, NY 11206.
Phone: +1 718-417-1118
http://www.robertaspizza.com/

Brouwerij Lane
78 Greenpoint Ave,
Brooklyn, NY 11222.
Tel: +1 347-529-6133
http://brouwerijlane.com/

Mini Book Series volume XXIV: Tour!

Brooklyn (part two)

It's a busy day, Monday, as I told you. I wasn't kidding. Still lots more happening.

Radio interview done, we've still a fair bit of time before showtime. Best not spend it all just boozing. I want my best legs on for later. A couple of the Brouwerij Lane guys invite us down to their new brewpub, which is just around the corner. Why not? I never tire of looking at shiny things.

The brewery is called Greenpoint Beer & Ale Co., though the pub it's in is called Dirck the Norseman. It's easy enough to spot, being painted Ikea blue and yellow. The brewery hasn't officially opened. That's in a few days. Luckily there's beer to try, a tasty Pale Ale. Now there's a tick - an unreleased beer. But only for a day or two.

Back at Brouwerij Lane, no-one is quite sure what time is showtime. There aren't many punters about. We decide that there's time for a quick meal. Dann, Martha and me. We venture out in search of Mexican. But stumble upon a Polish restaurant. That'll do.

It's called Karczma and has a well in the middle of the dining room. And the waitresses are wearing folk costumes. I always like that.

Mini Book Series volume XXIV: Tour!

They've a reasonable selection of Czech and polish beers, bottled and draught. Dann gets a draught pale Lager, I go for a dark one. Dann sniffs suspiciously at his beer, then tentatively tastes it.

"Dirty lines" is his conclusion. He looks at my beer. "I ordered the pale because that's more likely to be fresh. You've no idea how long a dark one might have been sitting around."

Thanks for raising my expectations, Dann.

This is my third meal if the day. Don't want to pig out, so I just order pirogis. Boiled, not fried. Martha has a plate-sized piece of pork.

I don't manage to finish my beer. Something that rarely happens.

It's much busier back at Brouwerij Lane.

"When do you want to start your talk?" One of the guys asks.

"Talk?"

"Yes, the 30-minute talk you're giving."

It's the first I've heard of it.

Mini Book Series volume XXIV: Tour!

"Dann, am I supposed to be giving a talk?"

"Did I not mention that? Just talk about historic beer a bit. It doesn't need to be too structured."

I frantically try to plan out a small talk, while chatting to various people. It's hard to concentrate on either. No point in waiting too long - I'll only fret more. Best just dive straight in.

Dann introduces me. The stove burns at my back. I clear my throat.

Suddenly, it's an hour and a quarter later. I've been talking that long, occasionally punctuated by questions. Not sure what I just said or how much sense it made. But they're clapping so it can't have been totally shit. And no-one buggered off half way through.

There's some book-signing and chatting to be done. As well as some beer-drinking. I'm relief drinking. There's even cask Mild. I can't pass that up. And more 1955 Double Brown on tap. Can't pass that up either. No reason I can't drink both. Though obviously not mixed. That would be weird.

We finish in Tørst, Evil Twin's bar. It's a bit relentlessly cool, both décor and atmosphere-wise.

We don't linger too late. Poor Dann and Martha have a ridiculously early start to dodge the New York traffic. Four in the morning they plan on leaving. My train to Philadelphia is a little after noon. I can have a nice lie in. And Tuesday is my rest day. Can't wait.

Mini Book Series volume XXIV: Tour!

Brouwerij Lane
78 Greenpoint Ave,
Brooklyn, NY 11222.
Tel:+1 347-529-6133
http://brouwerijlane.com/

Greenpoint Beer & Ale Co.
Dirck the Norseman
7 N 15th St
Brooklyn, NY 11222.
Tel: +1 718-389-2940
http://dirckthenorseman.com/

Karczma
136 Greenpoint Ave,
Brooklyn, NY 11222.
Tel: +1 718-349-1744
http://www.karczmabrooklyn.com/

Tørst
615 Manhattan Ave,
Brooklyn, NY 11222.
Tel: +1 718-389-6034
http://www.torstnyc.com/

Mini Book Series volume XXIV: Tour!

Philadelphia

Tuesday begins in leisurely fashion. Gazing vaguely at the TV in my undercrackers.

It's not an attractive sight, but no-one's there to see it. Washed, shaven and bekecked, I head up to the fifth floor for breakfast. It's billed as a continental breakfast. I don't get my hopes up too much.

If I liked cake, I'd be in heaven. Sadly I'm savoury to my core. I've only two topping options: butter or cheese.

At least I assume it's cheese. When I unwrap a slice the contents seem more plasticy than the plastic around them. Though it doesn't seem to make much difference whether I eat that or the wrapper, I plonk the cream-coloured putty on a slice of toast. Can something have negative taste? This reputed cheese seems to. Negative texture, too. It pushes the boundary of bland further than I care to go.

Not the best breakfast I've ever had.

I ask the hotel to call me a cab. I'm still waiting for someone to come back with that old gag "OK, you're a cab." but they never do. As I'd hoped, it's a car service rather than a yellow cab. I ask the driver how much it will cost to get to Penn Station. pretty reasonable is what it is.

The traffic is heavy and I've not quite as much time as I'd hoped at the station. I needed three things: a wee, some food for the train and a stiff drink. Not necessarily in that order. Though I did need the wee first. If an unfortunate trouser-soiling incident were to be avoided.

Luckily Penn Station had public bogs. Free ones. And not even filthy. Score.

I spot a TGI Friday's on the concourse and slip up to the bar.

"Is this seat free" I ask the nice young lady already sitting at the bar.

"Sure."

I order a double Jack Daniels. The young lady is drinking a cocktail. And has a ring in her nose. She's also reading a Kurt Vonnegut novel.

"He's a great writer. I loved his stuff when I was younger." I've only 10 minutes. Why not spend them talking to another human being? No chance of being suspected of trying to chat her up. I've only time for a few sentences and a quickly gulped dose of whiskey.

She's waiting for a train, too, unsurprisingly. Just had an interview at the publisher's Penguin. I tell her I'm in the US to promote my book.

Mini Book Series volume XXIV: Tour!

"What's it called?"

"The Home Brewer's Guide to Vintage Beer." I have to repeat it three times before she undertands it.

"It's your accent."

Been a while since I had anyone struggle with my accent. Though it happened fairly regularly when I lived in New York. I think I'm pretty easy to understand.

I'd like to eat on the train. I can't linger. The only reason I have any time left at all is that my train is 30 minutes late. At least that's what it said on the departure board.

I say goodbye to the nice young lady and rush off in search of food. A sandwich is all I need. I blow off my first choice when the queue appears immobile. I get served immediately at the next place. But have to wait to pay. Which prompts some grade-A worrying.

Pointlessly, as it turns out. They still haven't let passengers down onto the platform. I've some waiting to do.

"Have your tickets and id ready for inspection." That instruction was to cause me a good deal of panic in a few moments. But we'll learn about that next . . .

T.G.I. Friday's
484 8th Ave
New York, NY 10001
Tel: +1 212-630-0307
https://www.tgifridays.com/

Mini Book Series volume XXIV: Tour!

Philadelphia (part two)

Already on part two and I've not even left New York. Let's see if I can get all the way to the end of Tuesday this time.

"Have your tickets and id ready for inspection." They say. I obediently take out my verblijfsvergunning and hold it in the same hand as my ticket. It's a dead handy document, a verblijfsvergunning. I'm pretty sure they think it's a driving licence in the US. Whatever, they accept it as id. It saves having to take my passport everywhere with me.

The ticket inspector is only interested in inspecting my ticket. Waste of time getting out my id.

There are no free pairs of seats so I sit next to a middle-aged woman. I put my magazine ticket and verblijfsvergunning on my seat while I hunk my monster bag onto the overhead luggage rack. When I look back at my seat, the magazine and ticket are there, but the verblijfsvergunning is nowhere to be seen.

I check my wallet. No, I hadn't put it back. I check the floor under my seat. No. Under the seat in front. Not there, either. Under the seats across the gangway. No. I start panicking. And sweating. Just as well there are no security guards about.

I sit down nervously and do through my wallet again. No, definitely not in there. Where

Mini Book Series volume XXIV: Tour!

the hell could the thing have disappeared to? I check a wide area of floor, crawling around on my knees. This is bollocks. It's not as bad as losing my passport, but it will still be a pain in the arse getting a new one.

Twenty minutes into the journey, I'm still full of anxiety, anger and apathy. Where could it have gone? In a final despairing attempt, I stick my hand down the back of my seat. And out pops my verblijfsvergunning. What a fun start to the journey.

I get a taxi to my hotel when I get to Philadelphia. It's not far and only costs me ten bucks.

The strange covered-in bit of road outside my hotel looks familiar. When have I seen it before? I know - when we took the crazy Chinese bus from Washington to New York. This is where it stopped in Philadelphia. I'm in China Town.

Despite this being my free day, I have a couple of appointments. Most important is meeting George Hummel, who has arranged my event at Yards tomorrow. He's going to show me around later. First I'm having a few beers with one of my blog readers, Ed

Mini Book Series volume XXIV: Tour!

Draper, and his faincée Michelle.

We meet at Home Sweet Homebrew, George's homebrew shop. I'm a bit late, having got disorientated on leaving my hotel. We head off for the City Tap house. The weather is being weird. Having spent the last couple of days freezing my bollocks off, it's now warm enough to sit outside in the sun. Where we have a few beers.

I've mentioned on the blog that I'll be in the Nodding Head brewpub around 18:00, which I am. Another blog reader, Bill King, is waiting there with some books for me to sign. More beers are drunk.

Last time I was in town, I didn't have chance to visit Monks Cafe. For reasons entirely outside my control: a bus smashed into the front of it the day I arrived. Now I can see if it lives up to its awesome reputation. I break one of my most important rules: I drink a European beer. I've a good excuse. It's Tilquin Geuze, a beer I can't normally buy. And a cracking one, too.

I follow it up with a Pliny the Elder. Which goes very nicely with my mussels. George is very entertaining as he shows me his hometown. He's quite a character and seems to know every publican and barperson in town. Which is quite handy. We arrange to meet around midday the following day. For a few more beers while I'm waiting for the evening's event.

Which is what we'll hear about next time.

Home Sweet Homebrew
2008 Sansom St.
Philadelphia PA 19103
Tel: +1 215-569-9469
http://www.homesweethomebrew.com

City Tap House
3925 Walnut St,
Philadelphia, PA 19104.
Tel: +1 215-662-0105
http://www.citytaphouse.com/

Nodding Head
1516 Sansom St,
Philadelphia, PA 19102.
Tel: +1 215-569-9525
http://www.noddinghead.com/

Mini Book Series volume XXIV: Tour!

Monk's Cafe
264 S 16th St,
Philadelphia, PA 19102.
Tel: +1 215-545-7005
http://www.monkscafe.com/

Jose Pistola's
263 S 15th St,
Philadelphia, PA 19102.
Phone:+1 215-545-4101
http://josepistolas.com/

Mini Book Series volume XXIV: Tour!

Philadelphia (part three)

Breakfast isn't included at my hotel so I turn to Google Maps. There's a diner just around the corner.

It's in the indoor market. I somehow managed to miss that last time I was in Philadelphia. 30th Street Station excepted, there's not one place I recall from my last visit. It seems like a different town. I eat my usual egg and bacon combo. And drink an orange juice. Important to keep up the vitamin intake.

First stop in the Dock Street Brewery. Not that we stop, because it isn't open.

Instead, we go to Local 44 which is. Interesting. It looks like it was built as a pub.

Mini Book Series volume XXIV: Tour!

I'm reassured by the sight of handpulls. Unfortunately, the Yards IPA is off. I pass on the Bombardier. Not sure I'd even drink that in the UK, unless desperate. I have a perfumy IPA-type thing. I can't remember what it's called, but then again, I'm not trying to. This is my relaxing time, not my pointlessly obsessing time.

Mini Book Series volume XXIV: Tour!

After a couple we head back to Dock Street, which is now open. We chat with a brewer, then the owner. No, I can't recall what I'm drinking. I'm too relaxed.

The evening's event in Yards is a bit chaotic. One of the audience tries to take over my talk. Which is a bit annoying. I manage to wrest it back when he says something that's bollocks. Oh well. I sell a few books. And sign a few. I hadn't realised how early Yards closes in the evening and am a bit surprised when we get thrown out at 19:00.

Mini Book Series volume XXIV: Tour!

I pop in for some Dim Sum on the way back. Full of dumplingy goodness.

Tomorrow I head for Washington.

Down Home Diner
51 N 12th St
Philadelphia, PA 19107
Tel: +1 215-627-1955

Dock Street Brewing Co
701 S 50th St,
Philadelphia, PA 19143.
Tel: +1 215-726-2337
http://www.dockstreetbeer.com/

Mini Book Series volume XXIV: Tour!

Local 44
4333 Spruce St,
Philadelphia, PA 19104.
Tel: +1 215-222-2337
http://www.local44beerbar.com/

Yards Brewing Company
901 N Delaware Ave,
Philadelphia, PA 19123.
Tel: +1 215-634-2600
http://www.yardsbrewing.com/

Dim Sum Garden
59 N 11th St.,
Philadelphia, PA 19107.
Tel: +1 215-627-0218

Mini Book Series volume XXIV: Tour!

Williamsburg

I'm up early. Very early. My train is at 07:45.

I'm meeting Jamie and Paul at Union Station in Washington. They're driving me down to Williamsburg.

20 minutes before arrival, I think about adding Jamie's phone number to my contacts. Then notice that the battery is dead. Bum. This being an Amtrak train there's a socket by my seat. I start charging it.

Perhaps I should explain here about my phone. It's a US one Martha got for me. $6.95, with 200 minutes credit. A bargain. And dead handy, given all the travelling I'm doing. I start worrying about how I'll contact Paul and Jamie if my phone is dead. Do pay phones still exist?

My phone hasn't charged. And I'm too technologically-challenged to work out how to switch it on. Entering the station I'm gobsmacked to see a row of pay phones. They do

Mini Book Series volume XXIV: Tour!

still exist. Phew.

I won't go into all the excruciating effort it takes to contact Paul and Jamie. Let's just say that it involved two pay phones (the first turned out to be broken), a good deal of walking, the purchase of two newspapers and a good deal of freezing my arse off. The weather has turned cold again. And it's blowing a gale. But outside the station is still as dazzlingly bright as I remember. Last time here I was virtually blinded.

On the way down to Williamsburg we stop in Joe's Crab Shack in Fredriksburg to eat. I have various seafoody things and a Landshark. Followed by a Boston Lager. The beer selection isn't great.

After checking in to our hotel, we head for Colonial Williamsburg to see Frank Clark. He's arranged everything here and we'll be brewing together tomorrow. I'm dead excited about that. My chance to do some authentic 18th-century-style brewing.

Today I have some important form-filling to do. Including one that waives my right to sue, should I be maimed during the brewing process. Fine by me. A few possible scars for a unique experience? Even if the worst happens, Dolores will look after me.

We spend the evening in the Green Leafe Cafe, which has a decent range of beer. I drink various things, mostly IPA-like. Though I do throw in something Stouty for variation.

I don't stay up too late. Tomorrow will be an exciting day.

Joe's Crab Shack
2805 Plank Rd,
Fredericksburg, VA 22401.
Tel: +1 540-548-3844
http://joescrabshack.com

Green Leafe Cafe
765 Scotland St,
Williamsburg, VA 23185.
Tel: +1 757-220-3405
http://www.greenleafe.com

Mini Book Series volume XXIV: Tour!

Williamsburg (part two)

Breakfast is included this time. But there's no bacon, just sausage. I sob quietly as that horrible revelation sinks in.

We arrive in the historic bit of Williamsburg before opening time. Frank is there to let us in. We'll be brewing in the scullery of the Governor's Palace. It's pretty bare, just a fireplace, whitewashed walls, brick floor and a few wooden tubs.

We've time for a quick tour of the kitchen next door before we start. They're a cheerful and welcoming bunch who work in the kitchens. They get to make all sorts of fun food, only some of which gets eaten, sadly. The smoke house is wonderfully, er, smoky and the meat smells delicious. I feel like slicing off a slice.

The brewing equipment is pretty basic. Very basic. A copper pan dangling over a wood fire and a couple of half-barrel tubs. But first Frank makes some hot chocolate. They had great trouble getting hold of raw cocoa beans. Eventually they sourced them via Mars. It was worth the effort. The chocolate is delicious.

Mini Book Series volume XXIV: Tour!

Water is heating in the copper pan. We're cheating a little because we're using a thermometer. It does make sense. No point messing up the mash for nit-picking historical detail.

We're brewing a Porter. From a mix of grains, including some home toasted malt. I get to ladle some of the water into the tub. Then we tip in the malt and start stirring. A lot. This is when I discover exactly how to use a brewing oar. And realise the purpose behind its form. It's rather good at breaking up the clumps of malt that have formed. This so much fun . . . . as long as you don't have to do it all day, every day.

Once we've finished stirring, Frank has a go at capping off the mash with some malt. It's never worked before and the malt has just sunk. This time it miraculously floats on the top. It's blindingly obvious what effect it has. There's no longer steam rising from the mash. Heat is clearly being retained.

Mini Book Series volume XXIV: Tour!

We fetch sandwiches for lunch. And try some of the beers made commercially for Williamsburg, Stitch and Mumme. I really like the Stitch.

After lunch we make essentia bina - burnt sugar. It's quite a scary process. Brown sugar and molasses are heated in a small pot over the fire. Frank tells us that the trick is not to stir it. If you do, it won't ignite. The sugar plops and bubbles like lava then flames appear on its surface. Frank lets it burn a while then takes it off the fire and adds water to cool it.

Mini Book Series volume XXIV: Tour!

We're only doing two mashes today. There isn't enough time for a third. The wort is run off and more hot water poured over the grains. The first wort is boiled with the hops. After a while we add what's left of the essentia bina - I kicked half of it over the floor. The effect is magical. The wort turns pitch black after a couple of minutes boiling. Very impressive. There's also some liquorice root in the boil. Should make for an interesting beer. It's a shame I won't get to drink it.

I've a little time to kill before my talk in the early evening. I buy a pack of old-fashioned cards and wooden dice for the kids. Some lavender soap for Dolores. Then a beer and a couple of whiskies in the Dog Street Pub. Just to straighten my head out.

My talk is in a little theatre. It's the most professional venue I've ever spoken in. I even wear a radio mike.

I'm scheduled to talk for an hour. I manage to get through in just 80 minutes. Not bad going for me. It's a bit too technical for most of the audience, but the home brewers love it.

Jamie didn't sleep well and I feel sorry for her having to drive us back to Washington. We

Mini Book Series volume XXIV: Tour!

struggle to find somewhere to eat on the journey and end up in Golden Corral. All you can eat for $13. It turns out not to have been such a bargain. At least for me.

Governor's Palace
Palace Green St,
Williamsburg, VA 23185.
Tel: +1 800-447-8679
http://www.colonialwilliamsburg.com/do/revolutionary-city/tour-the-city/governors-palace/
http://www.colonialwilliamsburg.com/

DoG Street Pub
401 W Duke of Gloucester St
Williamsburg, VA 23185.
Tel: +1 757-293-6478
http://www.dogstreetpub.com/

Golden Corral
http://www.goldencorral.com/

Mini Book Series volume XXIV: Tour!

Washington

I awake on Saturday feeling a bit strange. And full of diarrhoea.

Jamie suggests we go to the Pancake House so I can work off my bacon deficit. Outside I feel worse. A lot worse. Soon the contents of my stomach are splashing all over Jamie's lawn. Just as well I was outside.

Breakfast is definitely off the menu as I head back to bed. With a bowl beside it just in case. It turns out my caution was well founded. My listless sleep is occasionally punctuated by bouts of vomiting.

This is worrying. I have an event later. I'm supposed to be talking and I can't even really stand. A real bummer.

I can guess the cause of my illness. It must be something I ate at that Golden Corral. Fortunately neither Jamie nor Paul ate any of the same things I did. They're both fine.

It had been planned for me to do some book-signing a couple of hours before the event,

Mini Book Series volume XXIV: Tour!

but that's cancelled. It gives me a little more time to recover. We drive over to 3 Stars in the late afternoon. I'm still not feeling great and doze in the car for an hour until it's showtime. It does me the power of good. I'm almost feeling human.

I do a little light book-signing and chatting. I'm not feeling great. Just about good enough to function. My stomach is behaving itself just enough for me to be able to take the odd sip of beer. That's good. Because it's sort of an integral part of the event.

We only work out what we're going to do just before it starts. It's a 30-second conversation between me and Jamie. BURP (Jamie & Paul's homebrew club) members have brewed six beers from the book. I put each of the beers into historical context, then the brewer says a little about how it was brewed.

It's a neat format. It gives me a rocky ledge from which to dive into the ocean of historical beer. From that fixed starting point, I wander randomly through the streets of the past, pointing out interesting sights as I go. It takes an hour or so, with me talking most of the time.

Once I'm done, I immediately feel totally exhausted. I struggle to chat, though there are plenty who want to talk to me. Including Catherine Portner, descendant of the family that once owned the largest brewery in Alexandria. With her sister, she plans opening a brewery making recipes from the original Robert Portner Brewing Company. It's an interesting project.

I really have to force myself to keep talking. I'm dead on my feet. Just as well I'd been able to sit down during the event.

Back at Paul and Jamie's, I have a bowl of turkey soup. It's the only thing I've eaten all day, other than a handful of crackers.

Let's hope I feel better tomorrow when we're off to Baltimore for the trip's final event.

The Original Pancake House
7703 Woodmont Ave.,
Bethesda.
Tel: 301-986-0285
http://www.ophrestaurants.com/

3 Stars Brewing
6400 Chillum Pl NW,
Washington, DC 20011.
Tel: +1 202-670-0333
http://www.threestarsbrewing.com/

Mini Book Series volume XXIV: Tour!

Washington and Baltimore

I awake on Sunday feeling much better. So much so that I suggest we go to the Pancake House for breakfast. I'm feeling back in a bacon mood.

The breakfast is pretty good. If slightly odd, as it includes bacon, fried eggs and a pancake but no toast. It's a bit weird mopping up the yolk with a pancake. We can't linger long as today's event starts at 14:00.

It's at a homebrew shop but has been organised by the Free State Homebrew Club Guild. Much like yesterday's event, home brewers have made some of the recipes. The format is the same: I improvise around the riff of the recipe for a while, as everyone samples the beer. It works well. And I'm in much better form, the food poisoning having been thrown off.

The turnout is smaller than yesterday, when I drew more than a hundred. Not half that number today. It's fun talking to an audience of home brewers. They ask intelligent, relevant questions. And mostly ones I have answers to. They're always the best type of question.

Someone has brewed a Grätzer. It's sour. Luckily the brewer realises that's not how the style usually is, so there's no need for me to rant. I tell him it's more like a Lichtenhainer.

I'm really happy that the 1839 Reid IPA has been brewed. Even happier when I taste it. There's that magical effect of a shitload of Goldings. It's a flavour I'm learning to love. When will a professional brewer pick that up? OK, Dann has done in the past with the 1832 XXXX Ale. But where is a regularly brewed beer stuffed full of Goldings?

Show over, I do a fair bit of book signing. And chatting. I'm more in the mood for chatting today.

When we're done, we head over to Victoria Gastro Pub for a bite to eat. And a few beers, obviously. The selection is pretty good. I go for something Paley Aley. I can't remember what exactly. And I wasn't taking notes.

Worryingly, there's a snow storm predicted overnight. I've got a flight to Boston tomorrow afternoon. I hope it flies. Wouldn't want to get stuck in Washington.

The Original Pancake House
7703 Woodmont Ave.,
Bethesda.
Tel: 301-986-0285
http://www.ophrestaurants.com/

Maryland Homebrew
6770 Oak Hall Lane,
Suite 108, Columbia, MD 21045
http://stores.mdhb.com

Victoria Gastro Pub
8201 Snowden River Pkwy,
Columbia, MD 21045.
Tel: +1 410-750-1880
http://victoriagastropub.com/

Mini Book Series volume XXIV: Tour!

Back in Boston

I'm flying from Ronald Reagan National Airport, which means I can take the subway there. I just need to change once.

There has, indeed, been 6 inches of snow overnight. But it isn't that cold, just about freezing. There's not a huge amount of disruption and flights seem to be operating normally.

As I'm already checked in, I only need to drop off my bag. But the US Airways bag drop off is pretty chaotic. I end up queueing with everyone else. It's a bit crap, really. As I've plenty of time. And my flight is delayed. Even the security check doesn't dishearten me too much.

I've time for a beer, and a whiskey, before my flight. So why not, eh? I've hardly drunk a drop the last couple of days. It's an odd feeling, knowing that the business part of the trip is over. There's a strange void. What should I do?

Boston is a great town. I always have a good time here. It just has one tiny little fault: the taxis are crap. As we pootle along through various tunnels, I suspect we're not going the shortest route. My suspicion is confirmed when we emerge into the light. We're down by a part of the bay not between the airport and my hotel. Cheating bastard. The driver doesn't get the usual tip.

Ensconced in my hotel room, I email Dann and Martha, asking if they fancy a beer or two this evening. They suggest Deep Ellum. I don't need any persuading. It's one of my favourite pubs, not just in Boston but the whole USA.

Given my hatred of Boston taxis, I consider walking there. But it's just a little too far. Bugger. I'll have to take a cab.

The taxi driver just about speaks English, or something vaguely resembling it. He hasn't heard of Cambridge Street. It's only one of the city's main thoroughfares. He tries to set off in the wrong direction until I point him the right way. He guarantees me the fare won't come to more than $13. That's reassuring. Unlike his knowledge if the city.

True to his word, the journey costs less than $13.

Dann and Martha are already inside. I'm surprised how awake they look. They had an early start (a very early start) and have been brewing at Buzzards Bay all day. For once, the brewday went like clockwork.

We eat a little cheese and sausage. And chat about beery topics. I keep thinking that there's something I should be doing, somewhere I should be. The trip has been so busy, that's been the case most of the time. I've nothing to do but sip, talk and eat. So much leisure is disturbing.

Mini Book Series volume XXIV: Tour!

I don't make Dann and Martha stay out late. I appreciate them making the effort to come out at all. Martha calls me an Uber cab. So much more pleasant than normal taxis. The drivers even seem to know their way around the city.

Just one day left. A totally free day in Boston. What will I do?

Deep Ellum
477 Cambridge St,
Boston, MA 02134.
Tel:+1 617-787-2337
http://www.deepellum-boston.com/

Buzzard's Bay Brewing Inc
98 Horseneck Rd.,
Westport, MA 02790,
Tel: +1 508-636-2288
http://buzzardsbrew.com

Mini Book Series volume XXIV: Tour!

Farewell to Boston

It's my final day in the US. My schedule is completely empty. What to do? I think you can guess.

I'm done with Boston taxis. I decide to take the T everywhere today. I start by walking to the tram stop closest to my hotel. Luckily my monster bag is lighter than when I arrived in the US. With all the presents I brought distributed, it's just full of dirty clothes and a few bottles of beer.

Cambridge is where I'm headed. To another of my favourite pubs, Meadhall. It's in the bit of Cambridge dominated by MIT and related industries. Plenty of people here with a few bob in their pockets.

I nip into the Coop before Meadhall. To buy some last-minute presents for the kids. I get Lexie an MIT T-shirt and Andrew a book about WW I. I know he'll like that and he needs a new book now he's finished the one about the Zulu War.

Mini Book Series volume XXIV: Tour!

Why do I like Meadhall? It's not just the beer selection, though that's pretty good. No TV's is what really makes it for me. Plus the food is tasty. And it's pleasant, airy space.

I continue my IPA theme. I start off with a Flower Power, then move on to All Day IPA. Let's see if I can do that name justice. I've several hours before my flight. Don't want to get legless.

I've mentioned on Twitter that I'll be spending the afternoon in Meadhall.

"Are you Ron Pattinson?"

"Yes."

My god. Someone has come looking for me. His name is Aleszu. He has some questions for me which I'm happy to answer. I always am. Very obliging chap, I am.

Mini Book Series volume XXIV: Tour!

I realise this is the first proper drinking session all trip. I slurp down multiple beers over a few hours and feel that warm fuzziness creeping up on me. I finish off the All Day IPA and have to move onto something a bit stronger. It's a pity they have no Dark Mild.

Taking the T to the airport is much less trouble than I anticipated. That's the last time I'll be taking a taxi to/from Boston airport.

My flight is overnight and as much of a pain as it always is. I get about 3 minutes sleep before I give up and go back to watching a film. I can't wait to get home.

Meadhall
4 Cambridge Center,
Cambridge, MA 02142.
Tel: +1 617-714-4372
http://www.themeadhall.com/

Mini Book Series volume XXIV: Tour!

II San Diego

Mini Book Series volume XXIV: Tour!

San Diego

Here I am. After a relaxing 16-hour journey.

How many things did I have to worry about today? A lot. Not all connected with the trip. My biggest fear was missing the connection in Houston.

It all went swimmingly. I would have even had time for a beer or two in the airport. Too knackered and relieved for that.

The final 3-hour leg from Houston to San Diego seemed to take for ever. But that could have been to do with my choice of reading matter: Government Intervention in the Brewing Industry.

I know. I had less geeky alternatives. Earlier. On the Amsterdam Houston leg I watched a series of shitty comedy films. Soul-destroying and time-consuming at the same time.

Then there was Private Eye. I'd kept a virgin issue to take with me. Quite a bit of it I gobbled down during my usual security shakedown at Schiphol. They pluck me out, grill me and sometimes make me to drop my kecks. Keeping my trousers up this time made me feel like a winner.

On the final leg to San Diego, the video programming wasn't free. The dry economic tome was my only option. When I could get my eyes to focus on the text. Not sure it would have been much more fun unblurred.

The immigration people in the US are much nicer. Pleasant, friendly. Though everyone is a bit sweaty after 10 hours crossing the Atlantic. My natural sweatiness is why they always select me for the underwear treatment in Schiphol.

I almost forgot; supposed to be telling you about where I'll be tomorrow:

Liberty Station
16:00 – 18:00 meet/greet and a book signing.

2816 Historic Decatur Road
San Diego, CA 92106
(619) 269-2100
http://www.stonelibertystation.com

I'll be signing my amazing new book. And chatting amiably with anyone who isn't an arsehole. If I have the chance.

Dropped by Ballast Point this evening. A bit disappointed that out of all their draught beers they only had one Dark Mild. Not really taking Mild Month seriously.

Mini Book Series volume XXIV: Tour!

Brewing at Stone

First, it's disclosure time. Stone and ChuckAlek paid my travel expenses and for most of the food and beer I consumed whilst in the US. For which I'm very grateful.

The two breweries are at about exactly opposite ends of the industry. Stone has two 120-barrel brewhouses, ChuckAlek a 1-barrel system; Stone started in 1996, ChuckAlek last year. That they are working together on a project says much about the camaraderie of the San Diego scene.

ChuckAlek have a series of one-off Porters and Stouts called, er, Archive Series. There's a new one each month. The recipes are interpretations (in varying degrees of strictness) of ones in Porter! and the Home Brewer's Guide to Vintage Beer. (Sorry, couldn't resist some tarting.)

Grant from ChuckAlek picks me up at 9 am. We're off to brew. A reasonably (but not stupidly) early start. Just as well. I only arrived at 5 pm yesterday, after a refreshing 16-hour journey. It's a wonder I know which month it is. I'm feeling quite chipper, oddly.

We're brewing at Stone Liberty Station, a brewpub in San Diego itself (the main brewery is in Escondido) which opened exactly 12 months ago. It's housed in a former US Navy training complex to the West of the city centre. With its cloisters, there's an oddly

Mini Book Series volume XXIV: Tour!

monastic look.

When we arrive the restaurant is empty, save for an army of staff, getting it ready for the lunchtime siege. The place is huge. Not quite on the scale of Munich's Hofbräuhaus, but not far off. The main room seats over 400 and there are several smaller ones, plus a big courtyard garden. That's one of the reasons we have trouble finding our way into the brewhouse: the place is just so damn big. They even have a courtyard with two bocce pitches.

Kris (Ketcham, the man in charge of brewing at Liberty Station) is already looking hot when we peer inquiringly through the window. He, literally, points us in the right direction. We have to go outside and around the back. He's already started the preparatory work.

I'm glad I checked the weather forecast before leaving Amsterdam. Usually, it's a pleasant low 20's celcius in San Diego in May. But an unseasonably early appearance of the Santa Ana winds has bumped the temperature up into the high 30's. Way too hot for me. Really low humidity is the only consolation.

The Santa Ana is to blame for the wild fires which have sprung up around the city. Once again I'm glad to live in rain-soaked Holland.

Mini Book Series volume XXIV: Tour!

Grant grinds the malt. I'm relieved not to be asked to hunk the sacks about. Sweaty work. It's English malt - from Crisps. Though the sacks of coloured malt also bear the name French and Jupps.

"That's very appropriate," I mention, "they used to supply London brewers with black and brown malt. It's quite possible that the original contained malt from the same source." I'm full of useless crap like this. "I'm pretty sure they were the last maltsters to make brown malt the scary way."

"Why did they stop?"

"Too many fires."

I realise I've forgotten to tell you what we're brewing. It's one of my favourite beers. For educational purposes. To bludgeon an historical point into a bloody mess. That much more Porter went to India than IPA. Barclay Perkins East India Porter from 1867.

Grant's intern Kaleb turns up to help. I get to play, too - some paddling in the mash tun. The easy bit at the start, when it isn't too thick. It's quite a hands-on brewery. One of the reasons Kris was glad to transfer here from the main brewery.

Mini Book Series volume XXIV: Tour!

It reminds me of something. My last foray into brewing at Colonial Williamsburg. I got to do some paddling there, too. Despite a couple of centuries of technological advances, brewing's core remains constant.

Once we've finished mashing in (at 153.9 F), Kris fetches us a blueberry and basil Kölsch straight from the filter. Slightly strange. It's a nightmare beer for Kris. Blueberry seeds clog his equipment.

"It's not very Kölsch convention compliant." I suggest. It's taken as the joke it is.

A worried Mitch Steele, head of brewing at Stone, turns up later than planned. He'd been stuck at the brewery until late, wild fires closing off his route home. Not that he's able to give us his full attention. A fire is within two miles of the main brewery. Every minute or so an email about the situation in Escondido bleeps into his phone.

We try an English IPA from ChuckAlek, which Grant has brought in a growler. Pretty good stuff. I wish I could remember which hops are in it[1]. I'm not taking notes, you see.

Mitch is bombarded with emails as the fire races towards the brewery. I'm surprised he can concentrate at all.

---

[1] Grant tells me the beer is called Trading Co. EIPA and the hops are Admiral, a newish British variety.

Mini Book Series volume XXIV: Tour!

In the grant, the wort looks as black as tar and nearly as viscous. Even in a thin tube, it's pretty much opaque. Brilliant. It tastes great: like over-sugared espresso, but more fun. I'm sure I'll love it. If I get to taste it. That's one of the downsides of cooperating on beers in distant lands. I don't always get to try the finished product.

When the wort is safely warming in the kettle, we go for lunch. Ribs and fish taco for starters, lobster roll for my main. Very nice. Not that you needed to know that.

Mitch continues to nervously check his emails. The fire is within a quarter mile of the brewery, he tells us. His relative calm impresses me. Worry trousers me would have struggled to follow the conversation. Or speak coherently. Hell, I struggle to speak coherently at the best of times. Or listen properly, my family would say. Bit of an attention deficit on my side.

Mitch gets a phone call: police have ordered the evacuation of the brewery. His meal finished, he hurries off.

Next I'll be doing my hop thing before roasting at gas mark nine for two hours in the garden.

Mini Book Series volume XXIV: Tour!

Stone Liberty Station
2816 Historic Decatur Rd #116,
San Diego, CA 92106
http://www.stonelibertys

ChuckAlek Independent Brewers
2330 Main St, Suite C
Ramona, CA 92065
http://www.chuckalek.com/

Mini Book Series volume XXIV: Tour!

Brewing at Stone (part two)

Right, time to describe the rest of my brew day at Stone Liberty Station.

Or rather describe the beers I drink with lunch. I kick off with the First Anniversary Ale. A beer, as it names suggests, brewed to celebrate the first anniversary of Liberty Station. It's dark and hoppy. They jokingly called it a black something or other[2]. Can't remember what, because, as I told you last time, I'm not taking notes. And my memory isn't what it was. It's fairly like a Black IPA.

I follow it up with a Go To IPA. One of the new breed of Session IPA.I quite like them, especially when, as today, I'll be boozing all day long. But they seem to really antagonise the more fascist end of beer geekdom. Why? Because in their narrow world an IPA had to be at least 6.5% ABV. Anything below that is an imposter. Like the wonderful 1839 Reid IPA (one of the recipes in my excellent new book), which only just scrapes over 5% ABV. Those dumb Victorian brewers.

Go to IPA is very drinkable and isn't messing up my head too much. What with the heat I've got even more of a thirst than usual. I take one with me back to the brewhouse, where Kris has delayed the boil so I can do my hop throwing in bit.

---
[2] Imperial Black Kolsch.

Mini Book Series volume XXIV: Tour!

When it's time the bung in the pellets, there's a nice head on the wort. It's even more impressive after the addition. Like the froth on the top of a cappucino. What are the hops? A load of Goldings. This is an India Porter, after all. In needs some company for its long journey.

We're brewing 10 US barrels and Kris will brew another 10 tomorrow. That's one conical's worth.

There are just two hop additions, at 90 and 60 minutes. That's what it says in my recipe, but it's just a guess. Few brewing records give details of hop additions. None I've seen from the 19th century. I made an educated guess, based on what brewing text books of the day recommend. Could be totally wrong. But as they weren't interested so much in aroma, more in preservative qualities, early additions make sense.

Grant from ChuckAlek gets to make the second and final addition. While his intern Kaleb gets to rake the spent grain out of the mash tun. I know which of the two I'd prefer.

Before I know it, four o' clock has rolled around. When my book signing is due kick off. It's in the garden. On the way to lunch I'd been surprised to spot a couple of punters out there. Anyone sensible was inside with the air conditioning.

Mini Book Series volume XXIV: Tour!

I'm set up at the back of the garden. Most importantly next to the bar and in the shade. It's still roasting, even out of the sun. Stick an apple in my mouth and you can have roast pork for tea.

I've plenty of time to consider my own mortality as, books arranged enticingly on the table, I sweat in a garden deserted save for the staff. At least I've a beer in my hand - more Go To.

Around 16:45, with brewing done, the others join me. Grant wants to try his own 1832 Brown Stout, but it's not on until 17:00. He decides to wait.

It's worth waiting for. A Lovely beer, full of chocolate notes, but finishing with a persistent bitterness. That's what you get from large early hop additions. A bitterness that lasts all the way to next Christmas, without ever jumping up and slapping you around the face.

As the sun drops lower and the air cools a little, more are tempted outside. But none of them pay much attention to my little book stall. The signing is supposed to end at 18:00.

My first sale is 5 minutes before that. I decide not to shut up shop but to carry on as long as anyone is showing interest.

I'm relieved when Mitch turns up. He's not been able to do much in Escondido. The police wouldn't let him anywhere near the brewery. But at least the fire hadn't reached it either.

We chat and drink and eat and occasionally I sell a book. It's even quite pleasant, once the sun is down.

"It's a day.", I say eventually. I'm back in my hotel by 22:00.

Tomorrow I'll be going to a museum and some breweries. Quite a few breweries. Including the main Stone plant in Escondido. If it's still there.

Mini Book Series volume XXIV: Tour!

California day three

Another 9 am pick up by Grant and we head off to Balboa Park. Heading for a museum, though there is a beery connection.

The museum only opens at ten leaving us some time to kill. Walking around the park slits time's throat pretty well. It's a fantastical place, filled with exotic museums and massive, contortionist trees. Many of the museums are housed in extravagant Spanish-style buildings left over from the World Fair of 1915. Including our destination, the Museum of Man.

It's currently hosting an exhibition called BEERology. About beer, obviously. Mostly beer in Latin America. Grant knows the curator and he gives us a little private tour.

There are impressive drinking cups - I'm surprised the golden one didn't get melted down by some conquistador looter. But best are the crazy South American growlers, in all sorts of highly-decorated forms.

The modern head-hunter beer drinkers sound even crazier. They have the longest word for beer the curator has found. Don't ask me what it is. It has about a dozen syllables and,

Mini Book Series volume XXIV: Tour!

as I keep telling you, I'm not taking notes. The head-hunter's beer is made from cassava roots and they get the majority of their calories from it - 80%. Each adult male gets through four gallons a day, women two gallons, kids one gallon. Just like Newark.

Next stop is Coronado Island. Which isn't quite an island, being connected to the mainland by a narrow spit of land. It's home to a big military base and some rather swanky housing. The approach - across a dramatically humped and curved bridge - reveals a perfect panorama of the city.

Our first beer of the day will be in Coronado Brewing's brewpub. Grant knows the brewer and, as he's not busy, we get a tour of the brewhouse. It's very cramped, in contrast to Liberty Station, though both are 10-barrel units. And built from copper rather than stainless steel. It's clearly seen a lot of use. In a separate extension out the back there are rows of conical fermenters.

We head back to the bar for a sampler flight and a chat with the brewer. There some pretty nice beers, especially their regular IPA. Very tasty. The food looks very tempting, but we need to move on. Back over to the mainland.

Mini Book Series volume XXIV: Tour!

Next is Monkey Paw, a low black box with a corner location. It's just after noon and boiling hot. Which is why it looks closed. On closer inspection, there's a note on the door saying they are open. They've just closed the door to keep out the heat.

It's very dark inside. Rather like a dive bar, which is what Grant tells me it used to be. A pretty insalubrious place, from his description. Now it's both a beer bar and brewpub. The brewing kit is hidden in another part of the building. Unfortunately, the brewer isn't around, so we can't take a look. He's off judging somewhere.

I get a sampler flight of Monkey Paw beers and a cheese steak with waffle fries. I thought cheese steak was a Philadelphia thing? As they have malt vinegar, I finish all my strangely-shaped chips.

Mini Book Series volume XXIV: Tour!

San Diego Museum of Man
1350 El Prado, Balboa Park
San Diego, CA 92101
Tel: +1 619 239-2001
http://www.museumofman.org/

Coronado Brewing Company
170 Orange Ave
Coronado, CA 92118
http://coronadobrewingcompany.com/

Monkey Paw
805 16th St,
San Diego, CA 92101.
Tel: +1 619-358-9901
http://monkeypawbrewing.com/

Mini Book Series volume XXIV: Tour!

California day three (part two)

We don't linger long in Monkey Paw. Just long enough to down four samplers and a cheese steak.

For the first time I'm heading out of the city. Our final destination is the main Stone brewery in Escondido. We have to drive virtually past the front door of another brewery, Societe. It seems silly not to drop in.

The location isn't the most exotic: a light industrial estate in a northern San Diego suburb. It's tucked away around the back, in a dull but functional single-storey building.

This is very much a brewery with a sampling room attached, rather than a pub brewery. Its kit is the largest I've seen so far and occupies most of the building, with just a slice at the front reserved for drinkers.

The number of samplers on a set has been different at every place so far today: 5 at Coronado, 4 at Monkey Paw, 2 here. Isn't there any industry standard for this sort of thing? Two hardly seems a set. So I get another when I've finished the first.

Like most of the places I've been in San Diego, the majority of the punters are young.

Mini Book Series volume XXIV: Tour!

Averaging about half my age, I'd guess. Does that make me the equivalent of two customers? Given the amount of beer I drink, it probably does.

The Imperial Stout is really good. As is the Dry Stout. Grant tells me the latter has won a medal. Or was it a few?

One corner is walled off and through a window I can see rack upon rack of oak barrels, all new judging by the honey tone of the staves. There are quite a lot of them.

"They're being patient." Grant tells me. "None of their barrel-aged beers have been released yet. Just a few teaser samples."

Samplers sampled, we're soon back on the road north to Escondido. There's no sign of the fire from the freeway. As we near Stone, there's still none.

We arrive without seeing a single burnt blade of grass. There are a few odd things about the brewery. Most notably there being no sign of any kind on its exterior. Not even the name.

Mini Book Series volume XXIV: Tour!

Everything looks so normal, it's hard to believe that the fire came so close. The only hint is a slight smell of smoke. They must have been cleaning like crazy because I know it was full of smoke and ash yesterday.

Mitch is still in an all-day sales meeting (lucky him) and another member of the brewing staff shows us around. It's ginormous compared to the other breweries I've seen. The two 120-barrel brewhouses working in parallel churn out more than 200,000 US barrels a year. The building is crammed full of towering conical fermenters standing shoulder to shoulder. A bit like that terracotta army, but with less elbow room.

Halfway through Mitch turns up and finishes the tour. I'm impressed by the number of firkins lying around. They must do a reasonable amount of cask beer. Come to think of it, I did spot half a dozen firkins perched on the bar on the way in.

Mini Book Series volume XXIV: Tour!

Packaging is in another building of about the same size. I'm intrigued by the automatic keg washer. Finally a piece of brewing equipment I've had professional contact with.

"It looks a lot less work than the one I used at Holes."

A highly skilled job, keg-washing used to be. Well, highly knackering. Especially lugging those 100 litre kegs around after they had been filled.

There's something weirdly fascinating about the machine that drops bottles into a case, folds the top shut then arranges the cases on a pallet.

"That's one of the machines we have the most trouble with." Mitch remarks.

The book signing is in the garden, where there are still traces of ash. It's pretty quiet. The fire yesterday has deterred drinkers. It's much quieter than a normal Friday.

I get to meet Steve Wagner, one of the owners, who seems a really nice bloke. We have a nice chat, while I shift a few books to the staff. Me and the bloke who runs the lab have an interesting[3] about beer analyses. He analysed lots of IPAs as part of the research for Mitch's IPA book.

---

[3] For me and him, but probably no-one else.

Mini Book Series volume XXIV: Tour!

"I'd been looking for regional variations in American IPAs. There are none." Mitch tells me.

At 6 pm Mitch drives me back down to San Diego where we're doing a radio show on 94/9, a rock station. It turns out me and Mitch have similar tastes in music, in particular a liking for sixties garage punk.

The show is great fun, with a pair of really funny guys presenting it. The off-air bits are even funnier than those broadcast. Though not all suitable for broadcasting, I'll admit. And we get to drink beer as part of the show. What's not to like?

Mini Book Series volume XXIV: Tour!

Mitch drops me back at my hotel about 21:00. It's been another full and enjoyable day. Just one full day left, but two more events.

Societe Brewing Company
8262 Clairemont Mesa Blvd,
San Diego, CA 92111.
Tel: +31 858 598-5409
http://societebrewing.com/

Stone Brewing Co.
1999 Citracado Pkwy,
Escondido, CA 92029.
Tel: +1 760-471-4999
http://www.stonebrew.com/

Mini Book Series volume XXIV: Tour!

California day four

I have a slightly later start on my last full day in California. Grant only collects me at 9:30.

We've a couple of events planned, one out at ChuckAlek's tasting room in Ramona, the other at the Beer Project in San Diego.

An unusual landscape rolls by as we drive up to Ramona. Literally up as it's 1,000 feet above sea level. Unusual landscape for me, I should say. Hills covered with straggly brush, some randomly strewn with boulders, resembling faces disfigured by some horrible skin disease.

Ramona itself is small and dusty, a chequer board of low buildings and empty lots. ChuckAlek is in a small strip mall, between a butchers and a Thai restaurant. It's not a town, being unincorporated. Not sure what you'd call it. A settlement, maybe.

Grant shows me around the brewery before setting up for the day. It doesn't take long. It's tiny. Especially compared to Stone, the last brewery I saw. I'm sure there are keen homebrewers with setups of a similar size. A couple of stainless steel tubs, some plastic conicals, a few stainless conicals and that's about it.

The kit is good for 1 US barrel and by brewing twice Grant gets enough to fill his 2-barrel conicals. The finished beer is mostly filled into sixtels (sixth of a US barrel kegs) though small amounts are sometimes hand-bottled. A good chunk of what Grant brews he sells in the tap room, either in the form of growler or drink-in sales.

The bar itself is small but cosy. A few bits of decoration. Nothing too fancy.

While Grant is swapping the beers on tap, the pancake man turns up. That's what we'll be eating for lunch. Yum.

Why is Grant changing the beers? Because, as a rare treat, all five beers (so far) of his Archive Series will be on tap. That's got me all excited. A chance to try five historic Porters and stouts. You don't get that every day.

Mini Book Series volume XXIV: Tour!

These are the beers, in the order in which they were brewed:

1850 Running Porter
1890 Double Stout
1880 Irish Stout
1912 Triple Stout
1832 Brown Stout

They're based, some more loosely than others, on stuff in my blog and books. After I've spent a good 30 seconds arranging my books in a tempting way, I get stuck into a sampler set of them. I tried the Double Stout yesterday and really liked it. Especially the chocolate-like brown malt character.

After Grant opens up at 11, drinkers start to dribble in. The home brewers make a beeline for me and start to chat. This is fun. A line of historic beers in front of me and people who want to talk beer. A couple of home brewers have brought along books for me to sign. Others buy a copy.

Crepes and beers slip down, chatter flows. I rather like the Triple Stout. Even better than the Double. Though all five beers are pretty nice.

Mini Book Series volume XXIV: Tour!

Just one event left and then it's back to Amsterdam.

ChuckAlek Independent Brewers
2330 Main St, Suite C
Ramona, CA 92065
http://www.chuckalek.com/

Mini Book Series volume XXIV: Tour!

California day four (part two)

I can feel my enthusiasm waning for these reports. I'm already busy worrying about my next trip. Oh well, here goes . . .

We leave Ramona in the late afternoon. We're heading back to San Diego for the last event. I'm giving a talk on Brettanomyces in British brewing at The Brew Project, a beer bar within a wine shop called 57 Degrees. It's a bit confusing.

On the way back we call by AleSmith, a brewery I've heard of. Not sure if I've tried their beer before. It's another light industrial estate affair. And definitely brewery with tasting room attached.

It's pretty full, packed with happy, smiling youngsters. Who are unlike me in every possible way, other than having beer in their hands. I'm a miserable fat old git, as I'm sure you know. But at least I'm not wearing a hat indoors.

Mini Book Series volume XXIV: Tour!

I get another set of samplers. A fourer this time.

What are they all again? Some of these:

Mini Book Series volume XXIV: Tour!

My brain is getting that fudgy feeling. Too many beers and breweries in too short a time for me to keep up. It's been an intense few days.

There are tantalising glimpses the brewery: a motionless bottling machine, the shoulder of a fermenter. But most of it is tucked well out of sight. I think I can live with that. I'm a little stainless-steeled out. It was fun seeing Grant's mini brewery. Not seen anything on that scale. Makes me almost believe I could one day own small but imperfectly formed kit.

On our way back into San Diego I spot a brick building that looks like a brewery. As we get closer I see "Mission Brewery" on the tower.

"It was one of the city's original breweries." Grant tells me. "Someone's just put a small brewery inside."

You trip over breweries all over the place here. 89 in all in San Diego, I've been told. Not sure if that's just San Diego city or the whole county. A hell of a lot, either way.

The Brew Project isn't far. Cavernous and mostly deserted. An art class makes up the majority of the customers. I'll be talking on the deck . . . . where it's still light so I can't use a projector. Nothing to do but get on with it.

It's not the greatest turnout, either. Just two brewers (the event was organised for the San

Diego Brewers' Guild). Their enthusiasm makes up for paucity of their numbers.

The talk is rather surreal as I can't show slides. There's greater degree of interaction with the audience than usual. At a certain point - I'm not sure when - it moves from a talk to a conversation. Quite a good one - conversation I mean - so I don't really care.

It's a strange end to a whirlwind few days. It seems like I've been here a month and like I just arrived yesterday. My sense of time is totally screwed. I've now got a 16-hour journey to look forward to. Then a couple of hours to wash and rest before a hospital appointment.

At least my life isn't boring.

AleSmith Brewing Company
9368 Cabot Dr,
San Diego, CA 92126.
Tel: +1 858-549-9888
http://www.alesmith.com/

The Brew Project
1735 Hancock St #1,
San Diego, CA 92101
http://thebrewproject.com/

Mini Book Series volume XXIV: Tour!

III Mid-West and Canada

Mini Book Series volume XXIV: Tour!

Toronto day one

Another tour, another set of travel reports to write. It feels like being back at school.

The little time I spend at home is now consumed by writing about my travels. Life could be worse. Every day could be much like the last. I should enjoy the excitement while it lasts.

My schedule is as punishing as ever, kicking off with two nights in Toronto. It's a city I've not visited before. Only my second time in Canada, too. My sole previous experience of the country was a few nights in rural northeastern Ontario. Where I brewed a beer at Beau's and hung out at their festival back in September 2012. I had a great time and unexpectedly got a chance to practice my French. But I'd not seen big-city life, other than rushing through the Montreal suburbs going to and from the airport.

I divvied up some extra dosh for more legroom on the flight out. Well worth it. I've no twat in front of me reclining his seat down into my lap. Plus there's just one seat next to me. There's so much legroom that the burly Russian sitting by the window can go for a leak without me needing to stand up.

I've brought Boak and Bailey's "Brew Britannia" with me. Travelling is about the only time I get chance to read anything long for pleasure. Though I do catch myself looking at the footnotes, curious to see their sources. That's not really what you'd do on a 100% pleasure read. Old habits are like Bruce Willis.

Once they get to the 1970's, they're retelling events I lived through. It's both slightly unnerving and highly illuminating to see them narrated in a coherent way. I thought I knew the story of the CAMRA's birth, but it turned out to be both more complex and character-driven than I realised. I noticed the tensions around the formation of CAMRA Investments without realising how deeply it split the movement.

The stuff about the SPBW was mostly news to me. I'd been aware of them, but, other than seeing their stand at beer festivals, they'd had little direct impact on me. Having learned more about them, I'm tempted to join.

Some of what was recounted form the 1970's really resonated with me. Like The first big national CAMRA festival at Covent Garden. It was in the summer I left school. Me and Martin Young, one of my classmates, made the trek down from Newark. It really did look as if the market had been moved out the previous day. We had to queue a while, but were lucky enough to get in. I recall drinking a pint of Yorkshire Clubs Dark Mild. The brewery was taken over and closed not much later.

It was another moment of bizarre recognition when a couple of places in Leeds were mentioned: CAMRA pub the White Horse and the Brahms & Liszt. I was once refused a drink in the latter for looking too much like a hippy. Sort of put me off it. I never had any trouble in the more down-to-earth pubs. Bloody yuppies.

Mini Book Series volume XXIV: Tour!

The description of the machinations around the Beer Orders was informative, too. I'd only seen the affair through CAMRA eyes at the time. And though "Government Intervention in the Brewing Industry" has since informed me of the big brewers' side and in particular Guinness's perfidious role, I'd heard little of the publicans' view.

The personal connection weakens after the 1990's, if only because, living abroad, I'm more remote from the British beer scene.

Hang on. This is supposed to be a travel report and I've ended up writing a book review. May as well throw a conclusion out. Well written - but I'd expect no less from them - and with loads of good stories about the individuals who drove the quest for better beer. It kept me entertained even while my arse was aching from hours of sitting.

I got a free copy, obviously. I'd have been pissed off if I hadn't, seeing as I had my publisher send them a copy of mine. Though I would have bought one as it's a pretty damn useful book for anyone interested in recent British beer history. And you know me. History is my thing. I've also met the authors once, exchanged multiple emails with them and my name appears in the acknowledgements.

Where was I before I wandered off? Sitting on a plane enjoying extra legroom. Let's continue.

I arrive in Toronto on time and start hunting for Peter Friesen. He's organised my Toronto event and offered to pick me up. Somehow we don't manage to connect. Me forgetting to charge my US phone before leaving didn't help matters. After a while of trudging around outside I get a taxi.

Despite being Saturday, it takes forever. Partly because Toronto sprawls so much - the airport is miles out, despite not being at the city's edge - and partly due to road works. Nearly an hour later, I roll up at my hotel.

The cab ride has left me with the impression of a schizophrenic city. On the one hand, there's the low suburban sprawl of houses and light industrial units. On the other, clumps of residential tower blocks, slowly forming into a forest around the lakefront and downtown. Like a combination of Hong Kong and Melbourne. Don't think I've ever been to a city quite like it.

Mini Book Series volume XXIV: Tour!

The hotel is in a rather grand 19th-century mansion. I arrive with not long to spare before an appointment with beer writer Jordan St. John. He's taking me for a tour of the city's cultural highlights. Only kidding. It's a pub crawl. At least I hope so. I've just about got my head sorted from the travel and time jump when he trawls up in the hotel lobby.

He suggests kicking off at Stout. Who am I to argue with a local? It's about a ten-minute walk away. On the way I get a chance to see a bit more of the city. Its schizophrenia is confirmed, with towering New flats alternating with remarkably English-looking Victorian terraces. Stout is a on a street of the latter, with tram tracks running down its centre. I think: "The kids would love this." Though maybe the kids aren't quite as into PCC cars as they were age nine. I keep forgetting that they're nearly adults.

Stout's billing as an Irish pub might have put me off, had Jordan not assured me of its good beer selection. It's pretty hot and we sit on the patio at the rear. They have a cask beer. Churlish to start there. Great Lakes Canucklehead. A golden Paley Aley sort of thing topped by a deep collar of creamy foam. Pretty effing brillarific. Especially as it's my first beer in a while.

Jordan shares my love of history, beer and beer history. We've plenty to chat about. He tells me about the book he wrote with Alan Mcleod on the history of brewing in Ontario and the new one he's writing by himself about the brewing in Toronto.

The Canucklehead slips down so sweetly that I order another. Food is ordered, chewed and digested while we wait for Alan (Mcleod) to show up. More beer is consumed, too. An Imperial Stout because, well, I'm on holiday and I can do what I want.

I'm easing into the day, Canada and the tour. Relaxation, like the beer, flows through my body like a low voltage electric shock. Only more pleasant. Just a few hours in and the fun is already palpable.

Mini Book Series volume XXIV: Tour!

Stout Irish Pub
221 Carlton Street East,
Toronto, Ont. M5A 2L2.
Tel: 647-344-7676
email: info@stoutirishpub.ca
http://www.stoutirishpub.ca

Mini Book Series volume XXIV: Tour!

Toronto day one (part two)

Alan Mcleod originally said he wouldn't make it to Toronto until around 17:00. Then an email arrived saying he'd be able to escape earlier than anticipated and should be hitting town in the early afternoon.

And sure enough there he is, as chatty and jolly as ever. He joins me and Jordan at our table, but doesn't join us for a drink. He still has his car with him. Being a lawyer, he wisely stays off the booze when any driving is involved. One slight problem. He needs to drop off the car at his hotel before he can start enjoying himself properly. And his hotel is out by the airport. Which is miles away.

Alan is gracious enough to watch me and Jordan continue to get our mouths wrapped around more beer while sipping an iced water. If only I possessed such self-restraint. I wouldn't be such a fat bastard, for one thing. We finally relent to Alan's sad puppy eyes and are preparing to leave when Peter Friesen arrives. Damn good timing, that.

I'm not quite sure why, but our plan involves Alan driving us all out to his airport hotel for car ditching then us all coming back into town in a taxi. On reflection it seems crazy, but I was a few pints into the session when I agreed. Beers has a way of making the oddest ideas appear totally logical.

The hotel is in a weird 1970's wasteland. A concrete colony of chain hotels stretched out along the airport's approach roads. Neither atmospheric nor particularly convenient unless you're flying. But it had one very important thing going for it: price. Alan couldn't find a reasonably priced room in the centre.

Mini Book Series volume XXIV: Tour!

After bailing out of our return taxi we rush inside Indie Ale House. I really do rush, having been beerless for more minutes than I care to remember. It's bright, modern and full of young people. I count anyone under forty as young, old fart that I am. I could be the father of every other customer other than Alan. Another odd feeling to stack up with the ones from earlier in the day.

Not that I've anything against this sort of thing. Youth hanging around in pubs, I mean. It's what I did when I was their age. Though I avoided places like this like Watneys*. I stuck to pints of Mild and the company of old men. But I've changed as I've aged. Mostly because that type of drinking experience isn't really possible any more. Also because I realise any culture without a constant influx of the young is doomed to wither and die as its devotees dodder.

There's a fair percentage of women, too. (Something else my youthful haunts lacked. Unless you counted barmaids.) Not that I find it odd. It's much like the trendier places in Amsterdam in that respect.

Tucked behind the bar there's a brewery. One of the shiny modern type I saw so many of in San Diego. Crammed into a space that seems just slightly too small. They must employ

Mini Book Series volume XXIV: Tour!

slim brewers.

I'm in pleasure mode and having fun, not scribbling frantic notes. What was that beer I just had? What's the one in my glass now, for that matter? It doesn't matter. As it tastes good and the chatter is flowing as freely as the beer, who cares? I certainly don't. Not as if the vast majority of you will ever get to try it, anyway.

It's still light when we emerge bleary-eyed and stagger off to the next destination, 3030. Look to the bottom of the page and you'll see why it's called that. Neither that imaginative nor memorable. It's a barn of a place, divided into two bars by a curtain. We head to the rear one, which ends in a stage, as it's the emptier. Bit of a mistake that as a band turns up and makes conversation if not impossible, more effort and less fun than I like. We decamp to the front room as conversation is the main reason we've assembled. Alongside drinking beer, obviously. But I don't need to mention that, do I?

Mini Book Series volume XXIV: Tour!

We end at another brewery, Bellwoods. It's popular. A bit too popular. We have to queue to get. I consider saying "Don't you know who I am?" to the nice young lady on the door, but think the better of it, anticipating a "No - now fuck off, you sad old git" reply. We eventually squeeze our way in and sit at a rustically rough table with a view of the shiny things. How much of the world's stainless steel is now tied up in brewing kit? A fair percentage, based on my recent North American experiences.

I get that paternal feeling again looking around the room. Do they have old men's bars this side of the Atlantic? Maybe hidden away out of sight somewhere.

Mini Book Series volume XXIV: Tour!

We eat some meat thingies and bread, served on a plank of wood. That wouldn't impress my son Andrew. He hates all the trendy modern food serving methods. "Can't they afford proper plates, dad?" is a typical comment. I'm more relaxed about this sort of thing. What's on it tastes pretty good.

Not sure what time I get back to my hotel. Midnighty-ish I think it is. I can afford to be fairly late. I haven't that early a start. My first event is all that's planned and that doesn't begin until the afternoon.

We'll be hearing all about that next time.

* Early CAMRA reference there.

Indie Ale House
2876 Dundas St West
Toronto.
Tel: 416-760-9691
info@indiealehouse.com
http://indiealehouse.com

3030
3030 Dundas Street West,
Toronto.
Tel: 416-769-5736
3030DundasWest.Reservations@gmail.com
http://www.3030dundaswest.com/

Bellwoods
124 Ossington Ave.
Toronto, ON M6J 2Z5
Tel: 416-535-4586
info@bellwoodsbrewery.com
http://bellwoodsbrewery.com/

Mini Book Series volume XXIV: Tour!

Toronto day two

It's Sunday 8th June, date of the first event on this leg of my tour. A homebrewers' event held, appropriately enough, at a homebrew shop.

Last night was a pretty late one. Midnight was really 6 am for my body. I'm impressed that I lasted that long. But when beer is involved my stamina is remarkable. I'm that dedicated a pisshead.

You can tell this hotel is an old building. I can feel the uneven floorboards through the carpet and there's plenty of creaking going on when someone walks along the corridor. Yesterday Jordan told me it was built as a home for the Gooderham family, owners of Gooderham & Worts, at the time one of the largest distilleries in North America.

The event isn't until noon, but is out in the boondocks, in Toronto's northern sprawl. It'll take a while to get there. Now 9 am. My mind is telling me to get up and go down for breakfast. My body disagrees: stay in bed, it's saying. A tricky one. Eventually my mind wins and I descend in the rickety lift.

I've noticed a trend in North American hotels. First time was in March in Brooklyn. You used to have to pay for breakfast, but did at least get a fry-up option. Always handy for calming the stomach and evening the shakes out of the hands after a heavy night. Now some hotels offer a free continental breakfast. Yippee, you might say. Except the food choice is extremely limited and . . . the plates, cups and cutlery are all disposable. Not exactly classy.

At a couple of these breakfast travesties I've found zero to eat, it being all jam and cake and flavoured yoghurt. Finding something I can theoretically eat often leaves me no happier: like the processed cheese less appetising than its plastic wrapper I encountered in Brooklyn.

They've got boiled eggs here, which is something. But the roll I lay it on is so dry I feel it sucking the last moisture from my already parched mouth. I abandon it and get more orange juice.

The Chinese girl on the next table is watching a film on her laptop as she breakfasts. Good idea. Distract yourself from the food.

I've still 90 minutes or so before I plan leaving. I use them wisely lying on the bed staring at the ceiling. Not really sleeping, more a stupor. I can't even be arsed to switch on the TV.

When I tell the taxi driver the address, he asks "Is that in Toronto?" "Pretty sure it is." He looks it up on a map. For quite a long time. He's struggling his way through the street index. I resist the urge to tell him that it's in alphabetic order. Eventually he finds it and off we head.

Mini Book Series volume XXIV: Tour!

"How long will it take to get there?"

"About forty minutes." Plenty of time to stare aimlessly out of the window, I think.

The suburbs to Toronto's north are no less sprawly than their sprawly neighbours by the airport. And no prettier. The roads are surprisingly crowded for a Sunday morning. I'll remember to avoid travelling around the city during the week. If this is anything to go by, it must be like Bangalore on a bad day.

Toronto Brewing at 3701 Chesswood Drive is where I'm headed. It isn't a single address so much as a small complex. Finding the right bit takes a while. We do some driving around until I spot a sign. It's hidden around the back. The driver forgets my box of books in the boot and was about to drive off with them until I stopped him. Sort of need those. That's the whole point to being here: selling books. Well, that and making friends and talking beer with people who genuinely want to talk about it. Unlike my miserable family.

I'm doing one of my standard home brewer events: I supply recipes and local home brewers brew them. The format works really well, especially for me as I get to taste the beers. Me getting beer is a pretty big thing. For me. I talk bollocks for a while, sorry, explain the historical context of the beer, the brewer says something about brewing it,

Mini Book Series volume XXIV: Tour!

then we all knock some back. Practical history in, er, practice.

They've brewed a decent variety: strong Mild, XXXXK, Grodziskie/Grätzer, Brown Ale, AK, No. 3 and IPA. There's even one in a cute little pin. It's a bit odd when customers pop in as we're doing our talking and drinking thing. I'm doing most of both, loquacious boozer that I am. The beers are pretty good, even the ones that really needed longer to mature. I'm happy to drink all of them.

Zack, whose shop it is, has arranged a table and chair for me to do my selling and signing thing. Which I do for a while.

I'd not expected food. The chicken barbecued on bourbon barrel chips is a welcome plus. Tasty stuff. I have two chunks, which is a lot for the new diet-conscious me. Not for the old gutsy bastard me, but I'm trying to keep him chained up in the cellar with Tarquin.

Peter Friesen offers to drive me back into town for a few beers. It takes a while. The traffic on the return is even worse than on the way. There seem to be a few design flaws in the road system.

It's started raining by the time we park up. I've no coat with me so we enter Bar Volo pretty sharpish.

"This is where craft beer in Toronto started." Peter tells me. It's been around for nigh on

Mini Book Series volume XXIV: Tour!

30 years, having been founded in 1985. Back in the dark days.

Another tiny brewery is somehow squeezed in behind the bar. Breweries seem as common as Bet Lynch around these parts.

I'm pleased to see not just a single beer engine, but a set. They've six cask beers in total, plus 26 kegs. Unfortunately, yesterday they held a cider festival and many of the taps are still pouring apple-based drinks. Never one to change hobbits, I order a cask beer, Punters Gold. English Golden Ale, it's described as. Can't fault that as a colour guide. Maybe a bit heavy on the citrus hops to be truly English, tasty though.

Peter has gone for a dry-hopped cider. His face tells me he won't be ordering another. Pretty weird, I think when he gives me a taste. Yeah, not sure I could drink a whole one . . . but I do. When I order the next round I inadvertently get one for myself. My own fault for paying more attention to the ABV than the description.

I hate wasting drinks. Even weird ones. It's not that bad. Just . . . odd, in a not totally good way. I finish it anyway.

We don't stay very late. Peter has a long ride home and I'm flying to Chicago tomorrow.

I walk back to my hotel. Oh look, what's that? Somewhere called Spirits. I quite fancy a

Mini Book Series volume XXIV: Tour!

whisky. The power of suggestion, eh?

"A Lug Tread and a double whisky, please."

"What type of whisky? We've a special on Jameson, $4 a shot."

"That'll do nicely. Straight up, no ice."

At the other end of the bar, two off-duty barmaids discuss men, music, waitressing embarrassments, random concert violence, and how effing cold it was last winter. "That's why I left Manitoba, weather like that."

Their chatter distracts me through a few whiskies then it's home and bed.

I'm so excited. Tomorrow I'll see Chicago for the first time[4].

The Clarion Hotel & Suites Selby
592 Sherbourne Street,
Toronto, Ontario M4X 1L4
Tel: 416-921-3142
http://www.clarionhotelselby.com

Toronto Brewing Co.
3701 Chesswood Drive,
Unit 115, Toronto,
Ontario M3J2P6
http://www.torontobrewing.ca/

Bar Volo
587 Yonge St.,
Toronto, ON.
Tel: 416-928-0008
http://blog.barvolo.com/

Spirits Bar and Grill
642 Church Street
Toronto, Ontario
M4Y 2G3
Tel: 416.967.0001
Email: goodtimes@spiritsbarandgrill.com
http://www.spiritsbarandgrill.com

---

[4] Other than O'Hare. Airports don't count.

Mini Book Series volume XXIV: Tour!

Toronto airport

I'm stuck hanging around in Toronto airport for a delayed flight. And annoyingly they don't sell any booze until 11:00. Should I be thankful that my flight is so late that time has now passed?

It's all very high tech. There's an iPad at very seat from which you can order without having to catch a waitress's eye. You can also use the iPad for other things. Like writing blog posts.

I'm having a Wellington Imperial Russian Stout. Canned, but pleasant enough. And a double Maker's Mark.

I wouldn't want the Stout to feel lonely, would I?

The delay means that I'll be late for my afternoon appointment in Chicago. I would tell you what it was, but the project is in a very early stage. Another of the 5 drillion projects I have in some phase of development. Like my book on malting, which might have been out by now, had I not been off gallivanting again.

I had some pretty decent beers in Toronto, most of whose names I can't remember. Cask caknucklehead is one I can recall. Excellent stuff, of which I drank several pints.

My reading matter is Brew Britannia. Been pretty good so far. And strangely unnerving when it describes events, such as the first big CAMRA festival in Coventry Garden, which I attended. Am I now part of history?

Mini Book Series volume XXIV: Tour!

Chicago day one (part one)

Time for the next journey. An international one, too. That's always extra special fun. Especially when travelling to the US.

I don't bother with breakfast in the hotel. My flight is at 10 am. I want to be there in plenty of time and I'm pretty wary of Toronto traffic, having seen the congestion at the weekend. Today is Monday. I decide to get a taxi at 7 am. I get an orange juice and a coffee while I'm waiting for the cab to trundle up. Breakfast proper can wait until the airport.

The traffic isn't as dreadful as I'd feared. I've still more than two hours until my flight leaves. But I immediately check in and go airside. Or at least start going airside.

It's all a bit strange. After I check my bag, it isn't whisked off on a conveyor belt but handed back to me. I'm told to take it off that way, so that's where I go. And find a long queue waiting for the security check. My favourite part of flying. There's a flight soon to Beijing, which explains the number of Chinese in the queue. After a while we're told to walk a couple of hundred metres to another security queue. Now isn't this fun. We're on a queue crawl.

We were told it was shorter. The queue, I mean. Doesn't seem appreciably so to me. There are several returns on the taped-off snake. I'm glad I showed up early. Why do I

Mini Book Series volume XXIV: Tour!

still have my checked in bag with me? One of the reasons for checking it in is so I don't have to lug it around the airport.

I picked up one of the US customs forms on the way to the initial queue. I thought I could fill it in before I got on the plane. So much easier when you're not crammed in an economy seat with the Samoan sumo-wrestling team either side of you. I realise why those forms were lying around and why I still have all my luggage when I emerge from security, my belt in hand and my shoelaces untied, to another queue. One for US immigration.

I'm actually pleased. For two reasons. The queue isn't that long. And it means I won't be pissing around after landing in Chicago.

The US immigration officials are always polite and often quite friendly. Quite a contrast with the bastards at Schiphol who keep picking me out for special attention. Ha ha, they couldn't get me this time - my initial destination was Canada, not the USA.

Right, all the official crap is out of the way. Time for some scran. There's bound to be somewhere selling a Full American. Always is, places like this. I decide to get as close to my gate as possible before my bacon and egg-based feast. There's a bar/restaurant on the right pier that's just the job.

Soon I'm staring wistfully over a plate of fried things at the planes outside. My mind is a wonderfully empty space, doing little but regulate chewing and breathing. Sometimes you just have to switch off. Especially when you schedule is as busy as mine.

I refuse a coffee refill. Time to get to the gate. It's surprisingly quiet, given the flight is due to leave in 40 minutes. I find a seat and start reading. After a while I get concerned

Mini Book Series volume XXIV: Tour!

about the lack of activity. Checking the screen, I see that the gate has changed .... as has the flight status. It's now "delayed awaiting aircraft" and the departure time has been pushed back an hour. I move to the new gate and continue reading.

The news doesn't get any better. It's the old trick of only slowly revealing how bad the delay will be. It starts as an hour and gradually edges up to two.

I wander back to the restaurant and sit at the bar.

"Double whisky, please."

"We can't serve alcohol before 11 am."

What? Never come across an airport, even in Britain, with that sort of restriction.

"I'll have a coffee, then."

The waitress remembers me from before and lets me have it for free. Guess my right to a refill didn't lapse first time I walked out the door.

There isn't even a gate assigned to the flight now. Where to sit? The bar is prickling with iPads, I guess. You're allowed to use them even if you don't buy anything. That's what a sign says. So that's what I do. Start fiddling with an iPad. I can check my mail. And write a blog post.

Other delayed travellers around me are doing the same, fiddling with iPads. After a while they start ordering drinks. First coffees. Then a bottle of wine. Which gets me thinking. Ordering is so easy. Just a few taps on the ipad and a Wellington Imperial Russian Stout and a double Maker's Mark are on their way.

Finally the delay stops increasing and the time to departure begins to tick down. The incoming aircraft appears to great rejoicing. At least in my heart. I may be only an hour late for my 2 pm appointment, if I'm lucky. Thankfully I've had a chance to warn Mike that my flight is delayed.

It's after 2 pm when we take to the air. I'm just glad to be on my way. And that I'll make that meeting. It's special because .... well, we'll discover that next.

Mini Book Series volume XXIV: Tour!

Chicago day one (part two)

I'm already late for my appointment when I land. No time to piss around. Thankfully there's no immigration shit to do, it's as if I'd arrived on an internal flight. I collect my bag and go directly to the taxi rank.

I've done my homework. I know exactly how much a cab from the airport should cost every city I'm visiting. No point getting stung unnecessarily.

It's a long drive. Through another set of sprawly suburban housing a low industrial boxes. I don't bother taking any photos. My hotel is to the north of the city centre, in Lincoln Park.

Working out where to stay in Chicago was a nightmare. I'd no idea of its geography. Where was a reasonable place to stay? I had no idea. After looking into the city's neighbourhoods (and checking hotel prices) I finally settled on Lincoln Park. It seems it wasn't such a bad choice. What finally swung it was seeing that the hotel was on what looked like a little High Street, with normal shops. Lexxie has given me quite a shopping list. This is where I plan picking up most of the items.

As I'm checking in, the desk clerk tells asks me if I want to take my box taken my room. I'm glad he reminds me of that. I forgot I had books arriving. "I'll pick them up later."

I hurry up to my room on the third floor, stick in the key and rattle the handle. Bloody door won't open. I try several more times before returning to reception.

"Had a little senior moment there, sir. Your room is on the fourth floor." Great. Extra delay is just what I need.

I stay in my room just long enough to switch on my flipflop and send Mike an email to let him know I'm on my way.

"1800 West Fulton Street, please." I say to the cabbie and I'm bouncing through the city again in no time. We take the motorway. Good thinking - it's a bit longer in distance, but much quicker in time. The final approach is urban, but in a low-key sort of way. Nothing much over three or four storeys. More New Jersey than New York. Though it does have a bit of Brooklyn about it.

Mike is waiting at the door of the brewery when I arrive. He's wearing an Augustiner shirt. Salzburg Augustiner, which is even cooler.

"Nice shirt." I say as we shake hands.

Mini Book Series volume XXIV: Tour!

It's Mike Siegel, one of the brewers at Goose Island who has generously offered to show me around. It's in a low, nondescript building much like the others on the street. In a couple of minutes, pausing only to give me safety glasses, he leads me into the brewhouse. You'd think after all the breweries I've been around recently that I'd be getting bored of looking at brewing kit. Nothing could be further from the truth.

I love hanging around in breweries, especially when I'm with brewers. They're always delighted to show off their toys. Me having an unhealthy interest in brewing equipment, I'm always happy to listen and learn.

On the first floor is the brewhouse. Like most I've been to recently, it's a smaller capacity than the fermenters, meaning they have to make a couple of brews of the same beer to fill one. 50 US barrels is the brew length, 100 US barrels the capacity of most of the fermenters.

We descend to the ground floor where the fermenting vessels, bright beer tanks and various other bits of kit are crammed into pretty limited space. Somehow they've found room for a couple of dozen oak barrels. They all appear to be full of sherry Bourbon County Stout. I wonder how much that little lot is worth? I'll probably never even see a bottle in the far distance, let alone taste it.

Mike takes me outside to show me the giant conicals they have there.

Mini Book Series volume XXIV: Tour!

"This isn't the nicest area. We had to build a wall and put barbed wire on the top. Before we did, stainless steel fittings kept disappearing." Mike tells me.

The building contains more than just the equipment to brew beer. The malts stores and the packaging department are here, too. The malts are stored slightly chaotically, pallets loaded with sacks piled several high. In the kegging room I show my usual bizarre interest in keg-washing machinery. There really is something wrong in my head.

Probably more interesting for geeks is our next stop: metal shelves packed with boxes of beer. Mike tells me that they keep a box from every batch for reference purposes. They've an impressive collection of Matilda. It reminds me of the one cellar at Fuller's, where they have bottles from every batch of 1845.

Now comes the fun part. Mike has some beer for me to try and Brett Porter, the head brewer, is joining us. There's an impressive array of their beers on the table. We begin with the lower-gravity stuff. Of particular interest is Matilda of different ages: one fresh, the other with a couple of years on it. Unsurprisingly, Brettanomyces has a much tighter grip on the latter. Almost a stranglehold on its flavour. Rather nice.

Mini Book Series volume XXIV: Tour!

They've kindly included a couple of Bourbon County beers: Bourbon County Stout, Bourbon County Coffee and Bourbon County Barleywine.

Bourbon County Stout is rich and luscious, an almost sugary sweetness offsetting the raw roast and boozy bourbon. I'd have another, if there was one of offer, but there isn't. I move on to the coffee version which is similar but with more coffee flavour. Not really much of a revelation, that.

I realise what a jammy bastard I am. I get to drink loads of rare beers, mostly without making the slightest effort. People just give me stuff.

Once we've done drinking, Mike takes me over the road to a warehouse they rent. It's stuffed wall-to-wall, floor-to-ceiling with oak barrels. I struggle to keep my chin off the floor.

We head for Hopleaf when I finally tire of looking at all that wonderful wood. For more beer, more talk, more fun.

Mini Book Series volume XXIV: Tour!

Goose Island
1800 West Fulton Street,
Chicago, IL 60612.
http://www.gooseisland.com

Hopleaf
5148 N. Clark St.,
Chicago, IL 60640
Tel: (773) 334-9851
http://hopleaf.com/

Mini Book Series volume XXIV: Tour!

Chicago day two

Nothing planned for this morning. Let's take a look at the shops. In particular Trader Joe's. That's a supermarket and I have a pocketful of food orders from Lexxie.

Invisible Kool Aid he particularly keen on. Pretty sure I'm not going to find that here. It's a bit of a hippy shop. And most of the stuff is their own brand. I get some chocolate covered coffee beans. A big package. Lexxie was really pissed off last time when Andrew polished them off. Plenty for everyone this time. I get myself a bottle of beer, too.

I pop into the smaller shop opposite called Milk & Stuff or something. Seems to be mostly cheese, booze and sweets. I see they sell spirits in ordinary shops here. Trader Joe's was selling it, too. You don't see that much in the US.

I've had an email from Ted Perez, who organised this evening's event. Do I want to meet for lunch? Sure. We agree on a sushi place close by. Nice and light. We have a very pleasant lunch, chatting of various beery things. You know how it is. Hard to stop once you get started. At least it is for me.

Ted can't stay long because he's working. I've still some time to kill before this evening's event. I go back to Trader Joe's and get another beer. Seems silly not to. A bomber of something IPA-ey. Nothing too heavy.

Tonight's event is downtown-ish. Me and my box of books take a cab. The weather isn't great: grey and grisly. I'm still trying to get a handle on the city. We're heading directly towards the skyscrapers of the city centre. To begin with. We veer right to skirt the downtown and get to the south, which is our destination.

Moxee Kitchen & Madmouse Brewery is embedded in the University of Illinois. A good spot for a brewery, I guess. All those thirsty students nearby.

Due to organisational difficulties (I left it too late) the format is slightly different. There won't be a set of homebrewed beer, but some De Molen SSS and maybe something else to try. Not 100% sure what.

After setting up my books in an attractive pile, I'm called over to the bar. One of the brewers from Green Flash is there chatting with the bar manager. He's trying to persuade him to take some of his beer. Doesn't seem like much persuasion is necessary. We chat a little and I persuade him to buy a copy of my book. Result.

The event is pretty low key. A bit too low key, perhaps. There is some homebrew. Someone has brewed a Younger's No. 1. They've even used the proper label. I'm dead impressed. The beer is pretty good, too.

Mini Book Series volume XXIV: Tour!

One of the audience, Mark Linsner, offers to take me around a few pubs when the event is done. We head off into the rainy night, with nothing to protect us but our thirsts.

We arrive at the **Map Room**. "Ron!" someone calls. Well blow me if it isn't Joe Stange. What sort of coincidence is that? Turns out he's also headed to Grand Rapids and the NHC. What a small world it is.

I'm not too late. My flight is at midday tomorrow. No need to be up too early. Which is how I like it.

Moxee Kitchen & Madmouse Brewery,
724 W Maxwell St, Chicago,
Illinois 60607.
http://www.moxeerestaurant.com/

The Map Room
1949 N. Hoyne
Chicago, IL 60647.
Tel: 773 252 7636
http://maproom.com/

Mini Book Series volume XXIV: Tour!

Mini Book Series volume XXIV: Tour!

Grand Rapids day one

I don't lie in too late. I don't want to be in a rush at the airport. I hate rushing, and especially at airports.

I take Monday's drive in reverse, down the same dully tan motorway. It's no prettier today. Nor are the rusting subway stations stuck between it carriageways. Occasional battered silver trains rock past.

I'm flying with United again. There's something disturbingly anarchic about self-service checkin in the USA. Confusion reigns. My confirmation number isn't recognised so I scan my passport, then enter the first three letters of my destination "GRA". I pick Grand Rapids from the list and it says . . . . it can't find a reservation for Mr. Pattinson for that destination in the next 12 hours. What?

I try again and get the same result. Then I realise I've been trying to check in on the hand baggage only section. I try the deeply anarchic checked in bag section. It's like a refugee column, bags and confused people strewn everywhere.

Eventually the Chinese youth in front of me finishes checking in and it's my turn. Where the hell has my booking gone? I scan my passport again and enter "GRA" once more. Hang on - there are two Grand Rapids in the list: MN and MI. I'm going to Grand Rapids MI, not MN. Silly me. I gratefully clutch my boarding pass and dump my bag.

I'd counted on getting some breakfast here at the airport. But I'm too late. Everywhere stops breakfast at 10 am. Seems a bit early to me. I have to make do with a hamburger instead.

I get to my gate but can't see any mention of my flight. That's not good. I find a screen and sure enough "Delayed - awaiting aircraft." Damn. Same shit as Monday. The gate has changed, too. I traipse off to the new gate. And wait. Isn't this fun?

I'm lucky. Today the flight's only a couple of hours late. Stan Hieronymus is supposed to be picking me up it 17:00 for a joint event this evening. Looks like I'll be just about there in time.

It's 16:45 when I drop my bag on the floor of my room. I've got enough time to put my toothbrush in the bathroom and quickly check my mail on my flipflop before rushing off to the lobby. Stan arrives a few minutes later.

Great to see Stan again. We've only met in the flesh once before, many years ago. Had plenty of email contact in the meantime. Steve Siciliano is waiting in a car outside. He's organised the event tonight out at Perrin Brewing, where me and Stan will be signing books. There will be a bunch of home brewers there with beer, too. Sounds like fun.

But first Steve takes us to look at his shop, Siciliano's Market. He sells not just home brewing supplies and but commercially-brewed beer, too. It's pretty neat. We can't stay long because we need to get to the brewery and set up.

"Do you need the PA?" Steve asks me.

"Nah, I don't think so. I talk pretty loud, especially after a couple of beers."

I change my mind after going inside. It's an echoey barn of a place and all the noise from the crowded bar rises straight up to the upper level where we'll be. I'll be on a hiding to nothing without a mike.

Home brewers start to trickle upstairs. They've got beer with them. A special beer that was brewed at a big outdoor event in a city square. Everyone got the same basic Brown Ale recipe but were free to play around with it by adding extra ingredients of leaving ones out. They're surprisingly diverse.

Stan speaks for a couple of minutes, then it's my turn. Twenty unscripted minutes on historic brewing. It goes OK, despite the din. I'm getting quite used to this, standing up and saying, sort of, "Buy my book." for a while. Well. not quite as upfront as that, but you get the idea.

When I've done talking bollocks, I flog a few books, sign rather more, chat, drink beer, meet people and do all the fun things you can do in a pub. Quite a lot of beer is drunk.

I don't get back too late. I've a breakfast appointment with the Langleys. We still haven't quite finished the talk we'll be giving tomorrow. Oh well, what's the worst that could happen?

Siciliano's Market
2840 Lake Michigan Drive NW
Grand Rapids, MI 49504
Tel: 616 453 9674
info@sicilianosmkt.com
https://www.sicilianosmkt.com/

Perrin Brewing Company
5910 Comstock Park Dr NW,
Comstock Park,
MI 49321
http://perrinbrewing.com/

Mini Book Series volume XXIV: Tour!

Grand Rapids day two

I've a busy day ahead. I jump in the shower and hurry down to my breakfast meeting.

I find Paul and Jamie already there. Paul is getting stuck into some oatmeal. I've gone for the healthy fried option: eggs, bacon, those potato things. It's only when I'm on holiday, is my excuse. True enough, too.

Paul is my co-presenter. We've still a little work to do nailing together our slides. Once breakfast is done, we head up to Paul and Jamie's room for the final editing. There's no rush. We've several hours before we're presenting. It doesn't take long to get everything sorted out. What to do now? Registering at the conference seems the obvious choice.

The conference is just a short stroll down the river from my hotel. The river is very swift. Wouldn't fancy dropping in there. Probably never come out again. It's called the River Grand. I think it may have something to do with the name of the city.

At the convention centre, I get my pass. It has a special bit stuck on the bottom saying "Speaker". As long as it gets me free beer I don't care what it ways. I pick up a bag full of stuff, some of it useful. Like a programme and a glass. Some of it - stickers and assorted bits of paper kack - not so handy.

Mini Book Series volume XXIV: Tour!

Wyeast have a little stand giving away beer. It seems silly not to have any. Gives me something to do with that glass. I arrange to meet Jamie and Paul back by the registration desk at 14:30. We're due on at 15:15.

Inside the hall, first thing I do is check out the book stall. Yep, they've got my book there. Even have a little shelf talker on it. Hope they manage to shift a few.

I wander around, pausing to look at particularly tempting shiny things. The miniature stainless steel breweries are a sight to behold. I find myself working out exactly where I could shoe-horn one into my flat. If only I could persuade Andrew to move out. His bedroom would make a perfect little brewery.

I manage to snap out of my brewing daydreams and get myself some beer. I didn't know what to expect on the beer front. Lots of homebrew had been my guess. But that isn't what it's like. Most is from commercial breweries, either sponsors of the event or beer bought by one of the sponsors. I'm not complaining. There's a whole array of Lagunitas stuff.

Which is an opportunity I can't miss, as the servers are from the brewery. It's a question that's been nagging me for a while. How do you pronounce Lagunitas? I ask the friendly chav with a beard behind the bar. I can't have been the first to ask. It's written on one of their labels. La-gu-NEE-tas. There's one mystery cleared up. Any theories of the meaning of life while we're at it? Thought not. Worth a try, though.

Various people talk to me as I trundle around the hall. Some seem to know who I am. I do, that's something I'm very strict about in my head, remembering who I am. Makes life so much simpler. Not really used to anyone else knowing, other than those people who hang around in my house. Family, I think you call them.

There is some homebrew to be had, in a special section at the back. I wander down there to try some out. I can discern no appreciable difference in quality between the professional and amateur brews. Not that I had expected to. I've had plenty of experience with American homebrew. Almost all of it good.

Our talk is in Grand Gallery A-D. One of the smaller spaces. Or should I say less huge spaces, because it isn't exactly small. It's slightly oddly arranged, with screens showing the slides either side of the stage where me and Paul are.

There's a reasonable crowd when we kick off. Especially considering we're not in the programme. Another speaker cancelled and we agreed to give our talk twice. Our real slot is tomorrow morning.

It goes pretty well. I get several laughs, which is always a good sign. Jamie's idea of holding up signs with the remaining time was excellent. I manage to finish just about exactly on time so there is time for questions. Oh well, job half done.

We hang around for the reception. Where we have a few beers and a bit of nosh before walking back to the hotel.

There's an event out at the ball park but we aren't going. Too much trouble and a bit expensive. Instead we head for a brewpub, Grand Rapids Brewing, not far from our hotel.

It's pretty busy and we have to wait for a seat. We have food, beer and not too late a night. We're on at 9 am tomorrow. Can't afford to stay out too late.

Grand Rapids Brewing Co.
1 Ionia Ave SW,
Grand Rapids,
MI 49503.
Tel: 616 458 7000
http://www.grbrewingcompany.com/

Mini Book Series volume XXIV: Tour!

Grand Rapids day three

My breakfast date is earlier today, 7:45. We need to be at the convention centre by 8:30.

I stick to convention and have bacon, egg and those potato things. With toast coffee and orange juice, of course. Sugar, caffeine and fat: all the major food groups. Paul unwisely sticks to oatmeal. Very unhealthy.

This time we're in a larger hall, ballroom D. It's not quite as weirdly arranged as yesterday, meaning I can actually see the slides on the screen. The crowd is bigger, but more subdued. It's being filmed, which has its up and down sides. Good that there will be a recording, shame it wasn't done yesterday when both me and the crowd were livelier.

Annoyingly, Stan Hieronymus was scheduled at the same time. Which means I've missed his talk. Bit of a bummer, that. A price you have to pay for being a participant rather than a punter.

I do a bit more wandering around the hall and get accosted several times while I'm on my eternal search for beer. I guess people know what I look like now. It's quite pleasant getting to chat for a few minutes with various people. I'm a sociable chap at heart.

Mini Book Series volume XXIV: Tour!

I've a book signing scheduled at the, er, book stall. Stan is on before me and has a huge queue waiting for him. Mine is rather more modest. Queue, I mean. Impressive when you think Stan has already been at it for over an hour. I'm surprised when I'm handed examples of my self-published books to sign. I guess a few must have escaped over the Atlantic.

I make sure to get myself a big beer before I start. Someone has given me the glass from the ball park do last night. It's at least double the size of the conference glass. Using it is a pretty obvious choice.

I'm the last author scheduled for the morning signing sessions. So no-one on immediately after me. I hang around for a while after my allotted time for any stragglers, a few of which do show up.

The afternoon sees the seminar I most want to attend: John Mallett (of Bell's) and Andrea Stanley (of Valley Malt) talking about making blown malt. Couldn't be more perfect for me. I'm dead jealous when I see that they're both in costume. I should do that myself.

The talk is as informative as I had hoped. And I get to chew some malt and drink beer brewed with it. Hard to think of a better use of an hour. I get chatting to John and Andrea when they've finished talking. They ask me out for dinner. Cool.

But before that I've a second seminar to attend. Jason Oliver (of Devil's Backbone) is giving a talk on Lager brewing. He knows a thing or two about the topic, having won several awards for bottom-fermenting beers. I had the pleasure of brewing a Barclay Perkins Dark Lager with him a couple of years ago.

I'd like to chat with Jason but unfortunately don't have time.

Dinner is at Grove, a foodie sort of restaurant. We all get a three-course tasting menu. What can I say, other than that the food is knockout. They've a decent beer list, too. The conversation, which roams around various historical topics, malting techniques and barley varieties, is totally fascinating. I rarely get to have beer chats of this quality.

That's not the end of the evening. Back in the town centre we nip into Hop Cat for a beer or two. And who should be standing at the bar but Jason Oliver. Isn't that a happy coincidence? He's chatting with Neil Spake, a long-time blog reader of mine. It's the perfect finish to a great day, as I get to talk Lager for a while.

Just one day of the conference to go. Unfortunately I'll miss the banquet. I'll be on my way to Chicago then.

Grove
919 Cherry St SE,
Grand Rapids,
MI 49506.
Tel: 616 454 1000
http://www.groverestaurant.com/

HopCat
25 Ionia Ave SW #100,
Grand Rapids,
MI 49503.
Tel: 616 451 4677
http://www.hopcat.com/

Mini Book Series volume XXIV: Tour!

Grand Rapids day four

Another day, another breakfast meeting with the Langlies. And another plate of fried stuff. For me.

I wander around the hall a bit taking a last look at the shiny things. And drinking more beer, of course. They're getting more generous with the measures, which is good. I get stuck into the Lagunitas beers. Then unwisely get a homebrewed peanut butter Porter. I only realise what it is after tasting it. Not a big fan of peanuts in stuff.

I've a very important appointment at 12:30. Mark Linsner, whom I met in Chicago has a very special treat for me. It's a beer I've read about, but never expected to get to drink:

Mini Book Series volume XXIV: Tour!

Ballantine Burton Ale. I'm eternally grateful to him for giving me the chance to try this legendary beer. Me and Paul and Jamie.

"Brewed May 12th 1946, bottles November 1966" it says on the label. That's quite an impressive bit of age. It's difficult to get the crown cork off. Which might explain why it's surprisingly well carbonated for its age. This what I scribble down as I sip:

"Sherry, butterscotch, wood and toffee aroma. Sweet/bitter flavour. Raisin, toffee, caramel and perfume aroma. Bitterish finish. In amazing shape for a beer that's older than me. No trace of Brettanomyces."

As a follow-up there's a 10-year-old bottle of Bass P2.

"Tar, toffee and liquorice aroma. Sweetish/bitter taste. Liquorice, treacle, raisin wood and alcohol aromas. Bitterish finish. Smoke, liquorice, treacle and tar aromas. Pretty nice, if a little thin. Definitely drinkable."

That's me done with tasting notes for another year.

The conference is starting to wind down with the final seminars taking place in the morning and early afternoon. There's only one I'm really interested in, Randy Mosher's about designing beer.

It's one of the better talks. Except it's clear that he has more than 45 minutes worth of material. Even rushing through the slides he still overruns. I get a chance to chat a little with him at the end. He seems like a really nice bloke.

He says one thing that really sticks. He mentions one of his family telling him: "Remember you're only beer famous." I'll have to remind myself of that. I'm several ranks down from beer famous.

When I get out, the exhibition hall is closed. Things are really running down. Paul and Jamie are in another seminar for a while. What to do in the meantime? Find a bar.

I don't have to go far. Reserve is just a couple of blocks away. It's a wine bar selling 100-odd wines by the glass. But they have a few decent beers. And more importantly a decent bourbon selection. I chat with the barman as I sip. He shows me a video on his phone from last winter. It's him outside the bar with a pan of boiling water. It's so cold that when he throws it in the air in turns into a cloud of ice particles. Very impressive.

Soon it's time to go. Not just from the bar, but Grand Rapids, too, I meet the Langlies to say good bye then jump in a cab to the airport.

After checking in I drop by the bar. They're showing the England Italy game. I get a beer, but can't eat because the kitchen is closed. By the time I've finished my beer the bar itself is closing. It's only 7 pm.

Mini Book Series volume XXIV: Tour!

The barman suggests I go airside where a bar will be open. It isn't. Well there are still people sitting there drinking, but they've stopped selling drinks. The England game is on. They're losing 2-1. Great. And my flight is delayed. Bloody United.

I don't have far to go when I get to Chicago. Just over the road from the terminal. I'm staying at the Hilton in the airport. I eat a hamburger in the bar and go to bed. I've a very early start. My flight is at 6:45 am. Let's hope I wake up.

Reserve
201 Monroe Ave. NW
Grand Rapids, MI 49503
http://reservegr.com/

Mini Book Series volume XXIV: Tour!

A few hours in Toronto

My wake-up call is at 4:45. I'm already awake when the phone rings.

I don't piss around. A quick check of my email then it's down to reception to check out.

I take the tunnel between the hotel and terminal this time. Last night I made a scary dash across four lanes of traffic, dragging my bag behind me. Not the kind of thing I want to do on a regular basis. Thankfully it's pretty quiet - not so surprising given the ungodly hour.

I go straight through to airside and head towards the gate looking for somewhere to have breakfast. It doesn't take long to find somewhere. I sit down and order eggs, bacon and potato things. Plus coffee and orange juice. Eggs count as one of your five a day, don't they?

There's something novel about this United flight. The bugger is on time. Not that it particularly matters, as I've hours to kill in Toronto. Around eight, in total.

An annoying amount of time, that. Long enough to make you contemplate leaving the airport, but short enough to make you wonder if it's worth it. And worry about getting to and from the city. Especially with my experience of Toronto traffic last weekend.

Fortunately, there's a simple solution. Gary Gillman, a regular commenter on my blog, lives in Toronto. I missed him last weekend as he was out of town. This seems like the perfect chance to finally meet. We've arranged for him to pick me up at the airport. Sure enough, there he is when I emerge from the terminal.

It's still pretty early and the roads aren't too busy as we head into town towards Gary's apartment. Once we get off the motorway, he explains about the neighbourhoods we're driving through. Toronto is a diverse place, that's for sure. I realise that I've barely dipped in a toe in terms of getting to know the city. Oh well, something for me to do next time.

Gary lives in one of the city's many residential towers. But one of the older ones. The view, as you can see, is pretty amazing:

Mini Book Series volume XXIV: Tour!

Gary has a load of Canadian beer and whisky lined up for me to try. We kick off with some retro beers from bigger breweries. They're mostly OK. Though anything is likely to taste good sitting on the balcony looking out at the Toronto skyline.

It's all very civilised. Definitely much nicer than numbing my arse in the airport. We have a pleasant light lunch with Gary's wife, who, like him, is a lawyer.

We've just enough time to take in one last pub, the Granite brewpub. He suggests it because they specialise in cask beer. You don't have to ask me twice if I want to drink me some cask. That thirst is never sated.

It's reassuringly pub-like inside, with lots of dark wood and a bank of handpulls. This will do nicely. I've obviously only seen a fraction of Toronto's beer scene. Not surprising, really, given the hugeness of the place.

We drink a little excellent cask beer then it's in the car and back to the airport. Nice to have finally met Gary. And to have done something useful with these few hours.

Mini Book Series volume XXIV: Tour!

In the duty free shop, I get a bottle of a Canadian whisky Gary had recommended.

I have a final Maker's Mark in one of the airport's iPad bars. Where I check my email and order bourbon at the same time. It's actually dead handy when you get used to it. The bar overlooks my gate. Also dead handy. I can wait at the bar until my group is called. Which is exactly what I do.

I do my best to rest on the plane. When I land at Schiphol, I'll have just enough time to go home for a shower and a change of clothes, then it's straight in to work.

Granite Brewery & Restaurant
245 Eglinton Ave E,
Toronto, ON M4P 3B7.
Tel: +1 416 322 0723
http://www.granitebrewery.ca/

Mini Book Series volume XXIV: Tour!

IV Pacific Northwest

Mini Book Series volume XXIV: Tour!

Seattle day one

I'm just back from my latest spin around the US. Nine days in the Pacific Northwest and Denver promoting my book. And, of course, meeting people, drinking and generally having the sort of good time only beer can facilitate.

It went pretty well. Like clockwork, really, despite a fairly complicated schedule, including four cities, three internal flights and an international train journey. I may finally be getting the hang of this stuff. I've learned from my previous trips. One thing in particular: don't eat in Golden Corall. Unless you like throwing up all day (I don't).

We'll start at the beginning, with me heading to Schiphol in a taxi.

When you fly to the US, you get an extra security grilling at the gate. I dread it. On my first two trips stateside this year they plucked me out, took me off to a separate room and subjected me to a minute examination of my baggage and a near strip search. They let me keep my trollies on, but that was it. It's a lovely way to start a long journey.

I've had a couple of calming whiskies at the bar, but I'm still apprehensive as I approach the security check. Try not to sweat, I'm telling myself. If only I really had that much control over my body. At the end of the process they attach a little sticker to the back of your passport. The agent looks at my collection and says with a wry smile:

"I see you've been through here a lot this year. And received special attention."

"Yes, I'm getting used to being strip-searched."

He smiles and waves me through. It's a good start.

The flight takes a northerly route over Iceland, Greenland and northern Canada. An icy wasteland of bleached beauty. At times it's hard to tell if the white expanse below is cloud or ice, save when a rocky mountain top pierces the white blanket. For once I wish I'd opted for a window seat. The bloke next to my snaps away for much of the journey. I'd have done exactly the same.

We arrive in Seattle at noon, leaving me three hours before my first appointment. Just about enough time to get a taxi to my hotel, orientate myself and get another taxi to the meeting point, Reuben's Brews in Ballard, a suburb to the north of the city centre. I've arranged to meet a few people there before heading off around other nearby breweries.

Reuben's Brews is tiny by any standards. It resembles a small car repair shop. A rollup garage door emphasises this impression. Despite its tiny size, the brewery also houses a tasting room which spills onto the parking spaces in front of it. I'm barely out of the taxi when I'm greeted by Don, who has soon pushed a pint of Alt into my hand. Ah, the first beer of the trip and my first in the Northwest. It slips down a treat.

124

Mini Book Series volume XXIV: Tour!

The other appointees trickle up and soon we've a small crew assembled, sitting between the fermenters and the mash tun. After a while we stroll down the street to Stoup, another slightly larger brewery only a couple of blocks away. It has a similar look, with a roll up door behind which are a few tables and chairs. It's large enough for you not to be sat amongst the fermenters. A mostly young crowd fills it up pretty well. Like most breweries I've visited recently, a row of oak barrels lie sleepily between all the shiny stainless steel. Does everyone barrel age now?

Our next destination, while still in Ballard, is slightly more distant so we drive there. Well, I don't do any actual driving. I sit in the passenger seat while someone else does all the work. This older brewery is different. For a start Maritime Pacific Brewing has a proper pub at its front, with a full kitchen. Though rather than a brewpub, it's a production brewery with an attached restaurant/bar.

It being Friday evening, it's unsurprisingly busy. Though the owner, George Hancock, takes time to show us around his kit, which is completely separated from the pub. It's a pretty decent size, with fermenters reaching up towards the ceiling. Inevitably, leaning against one wall is a rack of oak barrels.

Back in the pub, I drink a cask Double IPA enthusiastically. Rather too enthusiastically, given its strength. Cask is once again displaying its greatest advantage over keg: drinkability. Weird how many people say American-style IPA doesn't work on cask. I

Mini Book Series volume XXIV: Tour!

hold the opposite view: it really lifts them.

As I haven't eaten in a while, and despite my body thinking it's the middle of the night, I indulge in deep-fried battered bacon strips. I can feel my arteries clogging with every bite.

Maritime isn't quite the end of the night. Don drives me over to the other side of town where a brewery has just started up in part of the former Rainier complex. Rainier having been the local regional brewery, named after the volcano that looms behind the city.

Machine House, run by two British expats, concentrates on cask. Five handpulls stand to attention on the bar and there are no haunched keg fonts to be seen. My choice is easily made - they've got a Dark Mild. No way I'm going to pass that up.

Mini Book Series volume XXIV: Tour!

The industrial origins of the building are plain to see. It's stripped down to the point of being Spartan, but that might just be because it isn't quite finished yet. It hasn't been open long. Rough and ready, I'd call it.

And that's it for the evening. I'm amazed I've managed to stay up until 11 pm. And that my body doesn't think it's time to get up rather than go to bed. A nightcap of duty-free Laphroaig puts me in a sleepytime sort of mood and I glide peacefully into the land of nod.

Reuben's Brews
1406 NW 53rd St,
Seattle,
WA 98107.
Phone: +1 206-784-2859
http://www.reubensbrews.com

Stoup Brewing
1108 NW 52nd St.
Seattle, WA 98107-5129
Phone: +1 206-457-5524

http://www.stoupbrewing.com

Maritime Pacific Brewing
1111 NW Ballard Way,
Seattle, WA 98107.
Phone: +1 206-782-6181
http://maritimebrewery.com/

Machine House Brewery
5840 Airport Way S #121,
Seattle,
WA 98108.
Phone: +1 206-402-6025
http://www.machinehousebrewery.com/

Mini Book Series volume XXIV: Tour!

Seattle day two

I begin my day with a stroll to a nearby coffee shop for, er, coffee. The crusty-ish vibe of the place reminds me a bit of Amsterdam. Before all the yuppies moved in. Hang on. I'm probably one of those yuppies, aren't I?

I've an 11 am appointment at Pike Brewing. I'm meeting Charles Finkel, founder of said brewery, and Joe Walts of Narrows Brewing in Tacoma. I've an event there later today to which he'll be driving me.

As it's not far from my hotel, I stroll down there, taking in a little more of the city. The streets leading down to the sea are unfeasibly steep, like those in San Francisco. Thankfully it's only the last section of the roads. The rest of the city is reasonably flat. Unless, like me, you're used to dead flat.

Pike Brewing is just past Pike Place Market, a throbbing mass of indoor market halls strung out between 1st Avenue and the waterfront. I'm really tempted to have a quick look around. I love indoor markets. And outdoor ones, for that matter. But I'm running a little late. I don't want to take the piss.

Mini Book Series volume XXIV: Tour!

A polite young waitress asks me if I want to eat. "I'm here to meet Charles Finkel" She sits me down and goes off to look for him. I'd heard about the legendary collection breweriana. It doesn't disappoint. Every kind of object you can imagine: trays, poster, postcards, mirrors, glasses, bottles, bottle openers, statues - you name it. There's scarcely and inch of wall space not covered with some beer-related object. Dead cool.

I've plenty of time to investigate as the waitress doesn't immediately reappear. It's taking a while. Eventually she comes back and hands me a telephone. Charles is on the other end. Due to an organisational cockup, he's not on site. We have a brief chat and he seems a really nice bloke.

Joe hasn't arrived and I wait for him at the bar with a glass of Stout. Seems silly to sit beerless in a brewery. Definitely not the sort of thing I'd do. He apologises when he finally arrives. Heavy traffic has made his journey from Tacoma take much longer than anticipated. People coming into town have clogged the motorways.

We get shown around the brewery - the brewhouse shoe-horned into a tight space between the bar and restaurant - by a very enthusiastic and friendly guide. She tells us it's one of only two gravity-fed breweries in the USA. Downstairs where fermentation takes place, there's more room, though it's fairly well filled with all the shiny stuff you'd expect in a modern brewery. And, inevitably, there are oak barrels. Though also piles of golden

Mini Book Series volume XXIV: Tour!

gate kegs. Which I guess they're using as substitutes for casks.

Once we've given the brewery the once-over, we retire to the museum room to sample a set of samples. I'm amazed that Kilt Lifter, a Scotch Ale, is their biggest seller. I thought it was various shades of Pale Ale that sold best over here.

We would eat here, but it's getting late. The event at Narrows Brewing is scheduled for 3 pm. And we need to drive to Tacoma.

"We can order some food in when we get to the brewery, if you like." Sounds good to me.

We have a great view of Mount Rainier as we speed southwards towards Tacoma. It's a massive snow-clad volcano looming over everything. Tacoma is a fair distance from the centre of Seattle - about 40 km - but fortunately the roads are pretty clear.

Narrows Brewing is in the west of Tacoma on the, er, narrows. It's part of a marina complex that was once a saw mill. When we arrive Joe is relieved to see a barbecue stall outside. No need to order in food. I get a brisket sandwich with a side of cornbread. Really good stuff. The cornbread is incredibly dense, more like cake than bread.

There's time for a quick tour of the brewery before showtime. The equipment is very new and very shiny, but doesn't completely fill the space. There are fewer fermenters than you would expect. Lack of fermentation capacity is why we didn't do a collaborative beer. The explanation is simple: the building is timber framed and can carry a limited amount of weight, which limits the number of fermenters that can be installed. A 30-barrel fermenter filled with 30 barrels of beer is a fair old weight.

On the way into the bar I spot some familiar pictures of a bridge. One collapsing and I suddenly twig where I've heard of Tacoma Narrows before: it's the suspension bridge that twisted and tore itself apart in 1940.

There's a panoramic view of its replacement from the bar. Sadly my photo of it is too crap to use.

Narrows are releasing an Old Ale. It's a blend of Winter Ale which has been aged for a year in wine barrels with a fresh version of the same beer. They also threw in some Brettanomyces claussenii for that authentic aged flavour. I'm giving a short talk on Stock Ale, a topic dear to my heart.

There's a decent crowd of 40 to 50 by the time I stand up to speak. Not sure how long I speak. Once I open my mouth time seems to stand still, at least for me. Doubtless it's stretching to infinity for the poor bastards who have to listen to it. I get a couple of laughs, which is usually a good sign. And no-one throws anything at me, other than questions. I'm becoming surprisingly comfortable with public speaking. Not sure why. By nature I'm the shy, retiring type.

When the last question has been fielded, Joe takes a group of us down into the basement, where he has a few oak barrels full of maturing beer. Judging by how many of these things I've seen of late, the demand for barrels must be shooting up. I wonder if brewing will eventually soak up all the supply of second hand casks?

We share a few beers and a chat then Joe drives me back to my hotel. It's still pretty early. Which means I've time to drop by a Vietnamese restaurant I spotted earlier for a spot of Pho. It really hits the spot. I love me some Pho and I'm not disappointed. They even have some decent beer.

Once again a tot of Laphroaig gently pushes me into sleep's embrace. Goodnight Seattle. Tomorrow it's Denver.

The Pike Brewing Company
1415 First Avenue,
Seattle, WA 98101
Telephone: (206) 622-6044
(206) 622-8730
http://www.pikebrewing.com

Mini Book Series volume XXIV: Tour!

Narrows Brewing Company
9007 S 19th St,
Tacoma, WA 98466.
http://www.narrowsbrewing.com

local pho
2230 3rd Ave
Seattle, WA 98121
Telephone: (206) 441-5995
http://www.localpho-seattle.com

Mini Book Series volume XXIV: Tour!

Denver day one

I've tried to make this tour as easy as possible. Which is why my flight is at the very reasonable hour of 11 am. Why make myself get up in the middle of the night if there's no need to?

Though I've already got my boarding card printed, I show up pretty early at the airport. Why? General paranoia - I had a bad experience checking in with United at O'Hare airport in Chicago - and I plan getting breakfast there. There's always somewhere serving breakfast in an airport.

Once past security, I check a map to see what my dining options are. There's something called a grill that looks my best bet. But that's at another set of gates which is a train ride away. I'd rather stay closer to where I'm going to board, so I check out the nearby options. None sound very promising. First one I get to has a sign outside saying "Breakfast being served". A glance at the tables confirms that they have the egg and bacon style stuff I crave.

It's called Africa Lounge. That's why I hadn't been very hopeful of finding a fry-up. The name seems to only refer to the décor, which is kitschily African. I don't give a toss as long as I get my bacon fix. What to drink with it? Coffee, obviously, to wake me up. Orange juice for some vitamins. A double Jack Daniels because, well, I can. And that's what I usually tuck into in US airports. I order a second when I'm half-way through my food.

The plane is packed. I've had emails offering me $250 if switch to a later flight. No chance. At the gate they asked again a few times. The flight is uneventful so I liven it up with a couple of whiskies. I realise now how far out of my way Denver is - it's a 3.5 hour flight.

I've been to Denver before, back in 1989 when I was still working in the airline industry. The airport doesn't look familiar. Then again, after racking my brain for many minutes, all I can remember of the city is a steak house close to my hotel where I ate in a couple of times. It was much like the one where Homer Simpson attempts a steak-eating challenge. A 24 oz. steak - did I really eat that? I was a strange person when younger.

As my taxi bumps along the freeway towards town I realise it's a different airport. This one is much further out of town. Not that I expect I would have recognised the old one. I've been through so many recently that they're all blurring into one.

The weather isn't bad. A pleasantly mild 15° C.

I'm stopping at what looks like a pretty nice hotel, the Magnolia. It's right downtown, in a former bank. Sadly, the city centre is as bland and dismal as I remember it.

After opening my room door I pause for a while, jaw scraping the carpet. I've got a suite.

Mini Book Series volume XXIV: Tour!

It's bigger than most of my friends' Amsterdam flats. The kitchen is double the size of the one I have at home. Unfortunately, I don't have much time to appreciate it. It's already 4 pm and today's event is at 6. I've just time to nip to the 7 Eleven to buy some water and to discover that ordinary shops don't sell beer in Colorado.

Hogshead is already pretty full when my taxi drops me off outside. So full, that there are punters seated on the patio. It's warm enough for that. They've brewed a couple of my recipes: 1865 Lovibond XX, some of it in a wooden firkin, and a cask-conditioned Stout based on Barclay Perkins 1928 OMS.

Jake Gardner and Englishman Steve Kirby greet me when I enter. How did they know it was me? When I see my handsome face smiling out from a poster advertising the event, I understand why.

I'm impressed by the number of handpulls - seven in total. Steve tells me that 60% of their beer is sold in cask form. Or is "proper beer" as he calls it. I'm not going to disagree with him. I love me some cask. So I get stuck into some straight away. Really good stuff - properly conditioned, served through a sparkler and not too cold. I could drink it all night. Sorry, I do drink it all night.

After a while Todd Alström turns up with a pile of BeerAdvocate magazines. It's good to see him again. We always have a good laugh. There's a decent crowd again - must be at

Mini Book Series volume XXIV: Tour!

least 50.

By the time it's showtime, I've had time for a few pints. I speak better with a properly wetted throat. We attempt to use a PA, but it's picking up a radio signal that annoyingly chatters away behind me, like an unappreciative audience. It's a small, if crowded, room, so I do it the old-fashioned way: shouting.

After my 20-minute spiel (or was it 30? I find it hard to estimate, I get so caught up in the sound of my own voice) about the beers and historic brewing in general, it's time to get down to the serious business of selling books. Pretty quickly they're all gone and my money box is overflowing with dosh.

They've a food truck and I tuck into a barbecue sandwich. Just what I needed. I've had nothing to eat since my whiskey-accompanied breakfast.

A few of us stay behind after closing, shooting the shit and supping the cask. It's all great fun.

Tomorrow I've a free day in Denver. Todd has offered to share a few beers. Can't say no to that.

Africa Lounge
Seattle-Tacoma International Airport,
17801 International Blvd.,
Seattle, WA 98158.

Magnolia Hotel
818 17th Street,
Denver, CO 80202.
http://www.magnoliahotels.com/denver/magnolia-hotel-denver.php

Hogshead brewery
4460 W 29th Ave,
Denver, CO 80212.
http://www.hogsheadbrewery.com

Mini Book Series volume XXIV: Tour!

Denver day two

This was always going to be a quiet day. I've arranged to meet up with Todd around midday, leaving me the morning to myself.

I'm feeling a bit knacked, but need to get before 9:30 for breakfast. As it's free and includes bacon, no way I'm missing out on that. Fed, I go back to bed for another couple of hours kip. Why make life hard for yourself?

Todd messages me that he can't get away from work until later - can I meet him I Hogshead at 4 pm? No problem. I'm sure I can amuse myself for a few hours. What to do in Denver? I consult Google Maps and BeerAdvocate, then remember Falling Rock. It was mentioned last night as the town's top beer bar. And I'd spotted it from my airport taxi. Not that far away, lots of beer - a total no-brainer.

I notice something when I leave my hotel. It's effing freezing. It feels like it's about to start snowing. I though the cold weather wasn't due to sweep in until after I'd left. Evidently not. Wind, there's lots of that, too. I'm starting to wish I'd listened to Dolores and brought warmer clothing.

What's that hitting my face? Snow. It's bloody snowing! Brilliant. When I arrive at Falling Rock, I'm frozen.

Mini Book Series volume XXIV: Tour!

"Hello, Ron." Someone says as I walk through the door. Which is slightly disconcerting. It's the owner. He was at my talk yesterday. Thankfully. Not some random crazy.

I settle into a seat at the bar and we chat a little. He notices me looking admiringly at a Hammonds Ales sign.

"It's one of only two in the US." He tells me. "Michael Jackson was impressed when he was here. He used to drink Hammonds beer when he was starting out as a reporter. He recorded an interview here and insisted on having the sign in the background."

It's a cosy enough bar. The bar counter runs the whole length of one wall and the rest of the space is filled with booths. Breweriana is everywhere. Mostly in the form of bottles and tap handles, but there are also sign, mirrors and trays. I can never get enough of that stuff.

Some random dudes wander in and order beers.

"What about some shots?"

Mini Book Series volume XXIV: Tour!

"Yeah, why not?"

Why not, indeed? It is effing snowing outside. I'd join you, but I left my crazy head back in the hotel. I'm stuck with the vaguely sensible head.

For once on this trip, I'm taking notes. Here goes:

Odell's IPA
A classic US IPA - citrus, lemon zest, lemon, grapefruit. Slips down very easily for 7% ABV.

Comrades Super Power IPA
Similar flavours to the Odell's, but bitterer and just 7.6% ABV. Bit more grapefruity.

Boulder Shake Porter
Looks like it's on nitro. It really does taste like a chocolate milkshake, as the barman said. Slightly weird, but drinkable.

Great Divide Oatmeal Yeti
This stuff is effing black. The head is pretty dark, too. A stack of roast going on - fairly acrid. Some hops going on, too, but the bitterness mostly seems to come from the malt.

After a couple of beers, I need some food. I'm split between the buffalo burger and the Texas burger on a bed of jualapenos. In the end I go for the buffalo burger and ask for it with a bed of jualapenos. They're happy to oblige.

My favourite item on the menu is the Elvis Presley Memorial Combo.

"Two 1/2 pound patties cooked rare, topped with bacon, American cheese, 1/3 pound of pastrami, grilled onions, Swiss cheese, a fried egg guacamole & mayo on a big-ass bun. Served with onion rings, fries and a defibrillator. Price overinflated, just like Elvis. $46.40."

After a few hours, I head back to my hotel. It's now snowing way harder than is pleasant. More like specks of ice. Whipped by the wind, they prick my face like needles. Lovely. I'm not used to this sort of weather. It didn't freeze last winter in Amsterdam. Which is why there were so many bloody mosquitoes this year.

Mini Book Series volume XXIV: Tour!

It takes ages to get a taxi to go to Hogshead. Probably the change in the weather. It's caught a few people unawares. I see someone on a bike wearing shorts and another strolling down the street in a tee-shirt. Must be a random Geordie.

Todd, Steve and I share a few pints of cask beer. They sold two firkins of the Lovibond Mild yesterday. Not bad at all considering the size of the pub and the fact that they were selling several other cask beers. We get talking with a young baker. She's here because of her name, which is the same as one of the beers they brew: Julie Brown. We chat a while about the dreadfulness of American factory bread. She tells me of the revival in bakeries making proper bread. There are many parallels with the beer scene.

After a couple of hours Steve heads home and me and Todd drop by Lucky Pie for dinner. It's a combined pizzeria and beer joint. That sort of odd combination doesn't seem odd anymore in the US. Good beer is popping up all over the place. Like Copenhagen.

My hotel is within walking distance. But frostbite is nibbling at my grillox when I get there. I warm up in the hotel bar which, of course, also has plenty of beer options.

Tomorrow is just a travelling day, with Portland as my destination. Can't wait.

Mini Book Series volume XXIV: Tour!

Falling Rock Tap House
1919 Blake St,
Denver, CO 80202.
Phone: +1 303-293-8338
http://fallingrocktaphouse.com/

Hogshead brewery
4460 W 29th Ave,
Denver, CO 80212.
http://www.hogsheadbrewery.com

Lucky Pie Pizza and Taphouse
1610 16th Street Mall,
Denver, CO 80202.
Phone: +1 303-825-10
http://luckypiepizza.com/

Mini Book Series volume XXIV: Tour!

Portland day one

Today's flight is a little later, almost noon. But, the airport being miles away, I need to get up reasonably early. If only to catch breakfast in the hotel, which is free. No need to eat at the gate, which also saves time.

It takes me a while to find the United check in. Which is odd as Denver is one of their major hubs. Somehow I've missed a whole long row of bag drop offs. I blame the cold. In turns my brain to that thing that's sort of ice and sort of water. What's it called? . . . . . Slush, that's it.

I've got something called TSA pre. It means a slightly less humiliating security experience. You don't have to strip off quite as many pieces of clothing and disassemble your baggage. No idea why I got it, but I'm not complaining. Security checks irritate the arse off me.

With an hour or so to strangle, dismember and bury in a forest before boarding, I hunker down at the closest bar. It's called Pour La France! and has a weird French theme. You'd never have guessed from the name.

"Double Jack Daniels, straight up."

The bar is fringed with the like-minded. Loading spirits before boarding.

Airport bars are remarkably sociable. Knowing you'll part soon and never meet again, why not take a punt on a chat? I don't indulge myself this time, but watch others strike up conversations and smoke them to the fag end.

I mosey over to my gate at boarding time. Remarkably, my United flight is again on time. On my last book-flogging trip every single one was late. One very late.

This flight isn't total sardine time, but still pretty full. I indulge in a couple of whiskies. There's no in-flight entertainment: how else can I entertain myself in-flight?

My bag thunks onto the belt pretty promptly. Before I know it I'm cabbed and hotel-bound.

As the taxi crosses the Willamette River into downtown, I notice something odd. Portland looks like a city. A proper city, with shops and stuff. And those fleshy mammally, two-legged things I like chatting with. People, that's the word. I'm liking Portland already.

We pass a city square lined with ethnic food trucks. I've fallen asleep and this is all just a wonderful dream. Isn't it?

Bags dropped, I head for a nearby shop to get water. And in this case, beer, too, as Oregon doesn't have stupid laws. For a corner shop, the beer selection isn't bad. The

Mini Book Series volume XXIV: Tour!

prices are a shock. In New Jersey, bombers started at $6 or $7, heading north into crazy territory, before reaching totally fucking crazy do you think I'm a complete fucking idiot land. Here I can pick one up for under $3. Robbing New Jersey bastards.

There's a Deschutes brewpub just a few blocks away. I don't feel like going far because it's dead windy. On the way there I bump into a massive book shop, Powell's City of Books. It covers a whole city block. Another sign this is a cool city.

I slip in and search for the beer section. Easier said than done. The place is meganormous. But not particularly well signposted. After a few minutes of wandering I find it. Not bad at all. A stack of beer books. I'd give you a number, but do you think I'm the sort of sick obsessive that counts everything? [5]

Deschutes is pretty full, but I'm able to get a seat at the bar. Oh, look – they've got Fresh Squeezed IPA on cask. No long deliberation this time. It's rather nice, in a citrusy US sort of way. And a bit too drinkable. Before I know it my first pint is almost gone. Just as well it's only 6.4% ABV.

They're missing a trick, many US brewers and publicans. People drink well-kept cask more quickly than keg beer. And drink more of it. I'd be trying to push it to boost sales

---

[5] You've hacked my webcam, haven't you?

Mini Book Series volume XXIV: Tour!

volumes.

Though I notice a reassuring number of casks when I take the obligatory snaps of the shiny things[6]. It's a recurring theme in breweries I'm visiting. As with oak barrels, most have some. Maybe I was a bit hasty is saying they were missing the barge.

I order an Elk burger. Never had Elk before. It's also rather nice.

Three pints of Fresh Squeezed disappear in 40 minutes. No greater compliment than that from me. I'd happily drink another three. Which is one of the reasons I leave. Plus I'd like to visit more than one brewery today. Gotta keep to my quota.

Fat Head's Brewery is just a few blocks away. It's a bit of an industrial barn with a pretty decent-sized brewery behind glass.

Buuut . . . . . they've a cask Stout. A Julie Andrews (or is it John Coltrane?) of a beer for me. It's quite nice. Did I ever tell you of my youthful dreams of cask-conditioned Guinness Extra Stout? Not whimsical musings, things that pinged around my brain whilst sleeping.

---

[6] "This is boring, Ronald. Didn't you take any pictures of people. It's all brewing stuff and buildings."

Mini Book Series volume XXIV: Tour!

It's getting late, as my ramblings reveal. Time to ramble homewards, remembering to grip the camera better.

Laphroaig is my lullaby once more.

Pour La France!
B Gates
Center Core
(303) 317-9472

Powell's City of Books
1005 W Burnside St,
Portland, OR 97209.
Tel: +1 503-228-4651
http://www.powells.com/locations/powells-city-of-books/

Deschutes Brewery Portland Public House
210 NW 11th Ave,
Portland, OR 97209.
deschutesbrewery.com
Tel: +1 503-296-4906
http://www.deschutesbrewery.com/locations/portland

Fat Head's Brewery
131 NW 13th Ave
Portland, OR 97209
Tel: +1 503-820-7721
http://fatheadsportland.com/

Mini Book Series volume XXIV: Tour!

Portland day two

It's another leisurely start to the day. I quick continental breakfast downstairs followed by some lazing around my hotel room. I'm such a slob.

I've arranged to meet David Hauslein in the early afternoon at BeerMongers. It's a combined bottle shop and bar in a light industrial building. David's already there when I arrive and recognizes me. Maybe it's the box of books I'm carrying. We cosy up to the bar and set about the serious task of getting some peeve down our necks.

It's not a huge place. A few tables, some seats at the bar and fridges full of beer lining the walls. A smattering of customers here and there. Today's event – at Hair of the Dog – isn't until 4 pm, leaving me time for a decent session beforehand. Possibly too much time.

On the TV Holland are playing Mexico – and losing. Everyone is a little bemused at why I'm so happy Holland are getting stuffed. I'd even want them to lose if they were playing Arsenal, and that's saying something. Because, to quote Terry Collier, "I hate Arsenal".

Mini Book Series volume XXIV: Tour!

After a couple of hours of beer and beery chat, David drives me over to Hair of the Dog. Where Alan Sprints, who's organised the event, is waiting for me. It's another industrial type building, half of which is dedicated to the tasting room, the other half to the brewery.

Alan gives me a spin around the shiny thing room. Though it's not as full of those things as many breweries I've been to recently. No, here there are loads of wooden things. Quite a large number of oak barrels, most of which seem to be filled with one form or other of Fred.

There's a wide variety of barrels, all around hogshead size. What look like second-hand wine or bourbon barrels, Aardbeg ones from Islay and even brand new ones stamped with the brewery's logo. Barrel-ageing is obviously a big deal here. And by here I mean both Hair of the Dog and the USA.

Snuggling up to the oak casks are piles of dull and dented golden gate kegs in a couple of sizes. I've seen a lot of them this trip. I suspect that they're being used as firkin substitutes.

Mini Book Series volume XXIV: Tour!

The lineup of beers for the event is pretty impressive:

1804 Barclay Perkins TT
1848 Barclay Perkins TT
1931 Ushers Brown Ale
2014 Blue Dot
1839 Reid's BPA
1846 Truman XXXXK
1848 Younger 100/-
1916 Whitbread KKK
1860 Truman XXX (on cask)

All but the Blue Dot are from my book. Which I've started selling even before my short, impromptu talk.

It's another decent-sized crowd and they seem to enjoy my historical blether. Not sure how long it lasts again. I can keep on going for hours if no-one stops me. I love the chance of speaking uninterrupted. I rarely get that at home.

I shift most of the books I brought. It's a nightmare estimating how many to bring. I had to order an emergency extra box to be delivered to Vancouver. Took a bit of a hit on the shipping cost, but that's better than running out of books with a couple of events still to

Mini Book Series volume XXIV: Tour!

go.

I hang around for a while to chat and drink. Obviously the latter. When else will I get a chance to drink KKK? I never dreamt anyone would make a commercial beer called that.

Things are getting blurry. At some point we had back to the city centre, to Bailey's Taproom. I'm beginning to regret my early start. I polished off two bombers in my hotel before setting out. That may have been a mistake.

I suppose I walk home. It's not far.

No need of a Laphroaig eye-closer tonight.

Tomorrow I've a short flight to Vancouver. Hope I remember to wake up.

The BeerMongers
1125 SE Division St,
Portland, OR 97202.
Phone: +1 503-234-6012
http://thebeermongers.com/

Mini Book Series volume XXIV: Tour!

Hair of the Dog
61 SE Yamhill Street
Portland OR 97214
Phone: +1 503-232-6585
http://www.hairofthedog.com/

Bailey's Taproom
213 SW Broadway,
Portland, OR 97205.
Phone: +1 503-295-1004
http://www.baileystaproom.com/

Mini Book Series volume XXIV: Tour!

Vancouver day one

The weather has turned vile: cold, windy and a little snow. Great. I'll be making the hop to Vancouver in a little propeller aircraft which means I have to walk over the tarmac. It isn't pleasant.

For the first half of the journey, cloud veils the ground. It suddenly clears and a knife-sharp view of the coastal plain, backed by the Cascade Mountains, emerges. For once I've a window seat and I snap merrily away. As we near Vancouver, clumps of timber clot every waterway. Never seen that before.

The airport is fairly central and I'm soon at my hotel, Auberge Vancouver. It looks very posh. When I open my room door, my flabber is once again gasted: I've got another suite. Even nicer than the last in Denver, with its ridiculous views of the harbour and city. And there's my box of books sitting on the counter. What more could I ask for?

Mini Book Series volume XXIV: Tour!

My talk isn't until 7 pm but Jeff Longland, one of the home brewers who helped organise it, is picking me up at 1 pm. We're visiting a few breweries before kickoff.

We head for a part of town that used to be called Brewery Creek and is once again home to several breweries. We start at Main Street Brewing which, appropriately enough, is housed in a former brewery building.

The tasting room is simple, but functional: plain white walls and wooden tables with a bar area separating it from the brewery. It looks brand new, which in pretty much is, having been open less than a year. I'm excited to see four beer engines. (It's sad what gets you excited at my age. I found some fascinating turnips yesterday.) I opt for a Sessional IPA from one of them. I'm not making the same mistake as yesterday: too strong for too long.

The hate shit-balls thrown at Session IPA baffle me. Tasty beers you can enjoy drinking without fear of permanent brain damage. I'm as big a pisshead as the next bloke. And he's Josef Stalin. (Or is it Winston Churchill? I often get those two confused.) But sometimes a change of pace is a good idea. Or a liver transplant.

Mini Book Series volume XXIV: Tour!

We have a quick tour of the brewery, which is shinily impressive and was made not far away. They've already had to buy more fermenters to keep pace with demand. No oak barrels this time but lots of lovely new firkins. I'd take one home with me, but it wouldn't fit in my bag.

A few more people turn up, including Tak who's recently started brewing at Parallel 49, the town's biggest brewery. After Molson.

We're soon heading down the road to Brassneck, which is only a few blocks away. It's quite a different sort of place, though also quite new at just about a year old. The tasting room is very much about growler fills, which make up a big chunk of sales. There is no bottling.

Seating is at the rear, separated from the brewery by a collage wall of scrap wood. Great look.

In the brewery at the side and rear, things are much more cramped than up the road. And it isn't filled – though filled it is – with the usual stainless kit. There are three open fermenters and a wooden vat. Dead cool. I've seen neither in a North American brewery before.

Mini Book Series volume XXIV: Tour!

The odd firkin lazes between the fermenters. In the cold room there's one filled with 1987 Boddington's ELM and another with 1923 Courage Stout. Wonder where they got those recipes?

Before trawling up at The Cobalt, where I'm eventing, we drop by Pizzeria Farina, conveniently located right next door. It's a classy and simple, pizza joint. Not bad pizza at all. And they sell decent beer. What more could you ask?

The Cobalt is an old hotel with a colourful past, having long been home to "exotic" entertainment. It's now a grungy pub/music venue. It reminds me a bit of the Esplanade in St. Kilda, though without the glue-like residue masquerading as a carpet.

The event is in a side room called the Boxcar. It doesn't look quite finished. And isn't heated. On the upside, there is a screen and a projector, which is all I need. And three pins of beer. Two versions of Barclay Perkins East India Porter and one of Boddington's ELM.

Mini Book Series volume XXIV: Tour!

When it's time for me to do my talking thing there's a pretty good crowd - 60 or 70 - which packs the place out. It's an easy talk to give. I've done it a few times before. And I wrote it out of my head. I bounce off on a couple of tangents not really part of the talk as written. I usually do that, when I have time. I've a stack of good beer-history stories.

A few of us continue on to the Alibi Room for more beer and a bite to eat. I'm surprised that my hotel is close enough to walk to. Which is what I do when they throw us out.

A Laphroaig is again my late-night travelling companion to the land of dreams.

Main Street Brewing
261 E 7th Ave,
Vancouver,
BC V5T 0B4.
Phone: +1 604-336-7711
http://mainstreetbeer.ca/

Brassneck Brewery
2148 Main St,
Vancouver,
BC V5T 3C5.
Phone: +1 604-259-7686
http://brassneck.ca/

Pizzeria Farina
915 Main St
Vancouver,
BC V6A 2V8.
Phone: +1 604-681-9334
http://www.pizzeriafarina.com/

Cobalt Hotel
917 Main St,
Vancouver.
Phone: +1 604-685-2825
http://www.thecobalt.ca/

Alibi Room
157 Alexander St
Vancouver,
BC V6A 1B8.
Phone: +1 604-623-3383
http://www.alibi.ca

Mini Book Series volume XXIV: Tour!

Vancouver day two

I've arranged to meet Tak pretty early - 09:30. Just as well I didn't get hammered yesterday. We're going to do a small brew on a tiny pilot system at Parallel 49.

The view from my bed is incredible. I sort of wish I had more time just lounging around in my suite, it's so nice. See what you think of the view:

Our first call is a food truck for breakfast. As you can see, it's a beautiful sunny day again. Everyone keeps telling me how untypical it as for this time of year. I'm not complaining.

Fed we head for Steamworks, a brewpub where Tak worked until recently. As it's not yet open, we enter through the back.

The brewery is in the basement, just about touching distance from the nearest tables. I guess they have to be careful not to accidentally scald any diners. I get a quick tour of the cramped equipment then a chance to sample some of the beers. Tak meanwhile loads up with ingredients for our brew later that day.

Mini Book Series volume XXIV: Tour!

While he's busy collecting the malt and hops, I watch Scotland vs. Ireland a little. Who do I want to win? Difficult one that. I'll get back to you later.

We take a bus over to where Tak currently works, Parallel 49 Brewing. It's a good bit bigger than any of the breweries I've seen so far in Vancouver. Bigger than any on the whole trip. It covers several buildings, all crammed full of stuff, be it brewhouse, fermenters, packaging equipment or stock. It's hard to believe it's only a few years old.

The tour takes longer than most I've done. Logical enough, as it's so big. Sure enough there are both oak barrels and cute little metal firkins.

We dive into the tasting room for a beer or two. They've dead impressive counter-pressure growler fillers. It's doing a brisk trade in growlers and bottles.

Mini Book Series volume XXIV: Tour!

It's cask day and I'm asked to tap the barrel. I'm slightly reluctant remembering the incident with a 10-litre barrel of Schumacher Alt in our old flat. I didn't get the tap properly in and sprayed our living room with beer. After that, I was only allowed to tap barrels in the bath. It works fine this time, thankfully.

The half-barrel pilot plant has only just been delivered and the manufacturer is helping to assemble it and explain how it works. It's incredibly compact. I could easily fit it into my flat. Which starts me daydreaming. Until I imagine Dolores's reaction to me turning up with $3,000-odd worth of brewing equipment. No way that will fly.

It's got a bit late to brew. We decide to drop by the nearby Storm Brewing for a quick beer then to get something to eat. It's a good idea to eat at least two meals a day, I've realised.

I've been around a few breweries in my life. But never one like Storm. I'm told the owner built it himself. I can believe that. It looks like a pile of scrap metal. So ramshackle that I'm shocked when I taste the beer. Pretty good. How on earth can he brew in here? The "tasting room" is really just the space between the scrap.

Mini Book Series volume XXIV: Tour!

The owner is as characterful as his brewery. We chat a little and he gives us some distilled thing. Not quite sure what it is, but it warms me nicely for the upcoming journey.

It takes a while to flag down a cab. Making me appreciate that final warming drink. We're headed for an English-style pub. But it's packed. No chance of finding a seat. Instead we go to one of the Japanese restaurants nearby. The food is outstanding. The best of the whole trip.

The day ends with a Laphroaig brain-relaxer and a dreamy view over the bay.

Steamworks
375 Water St,
Vancouver,
BC V6B 1B8.
Phone: +1 604-689-2739
http://steamworks.com/

Mini Book Series volume XXIV: Tour!

Parallel 49 Brewing
1950 Triumph St,
Vancouver,
BC V5L 1K5.
Phone: +1 604-558-2739
http://parallel49brewing.com/

Storm Brewing
310 Commercial Drive,
Vancouver, BC, Canada
Phone: +1 604-255-9119
http://www.stormbrewing.org/

Mini Book Series volume XXIV: Tour!

Seattle day three

I've an early start. A very early start. I'm taking the train to Seattle and it leaves at 6.30 am.

But, as it's an international train, I need to be at the station an hour before departure. I ask for a 4.15 am wake-up call.

I buy myself a sandwich, drink and bag of crisps. That'll do as breakfast. I get a Canadian history magazine for Andrew as well.

Once through US immigration, I settle into my assigned seat. It's still dark when we pull out of the station. It takes longer than I anticipated – about two hours – until we reach the US border. Just before we get there, I spot two bald eagles sitting in a tree by the trackside.

At the border, we're told to remain in our seats while border guards come around the train to check passports and collect our customs declaration forms. It doesn't take long – not more than 15 minutes.

The train mostly hugs the coast, a vista of wooded hills and mirror-calm water slowly unfolding beyond the window. Occasionally the tracks dart inland, across flat, fertile plains of farmland. It's one of the most scenic train rides I've had in a while.

We get to King Street station on time and Jim Jamison is there to collect me. I've an event in his brewery, Foggy Noggin, in Bothell this evening.

Mini Book Series volume XXIV: Tour!

"Do you want to get some lunch?" He asks.

My sandwich has long since worn off: "Sure."

We go a place just around the corner, an Irish pub called Fado. I order a Lagunitas IPA and corned beef hash. Both are rather pleasant. Though the IPA comes in a jam jar. A Lagunitas-branded jam jar. Not quite sure why they serve beer in things like this. What's wrong with a proper glass?

I ask Jim if we can stop by a supermarket. "I need to get cookie mix and Kool Aid for my son." Jim is slightly bemused by Alexei's request.

When we're at the checkout the woman in front of us asks if we're getting the Kool Aid to dye hair. "Four packets of the Dark Cherry in boiling water. That's how I dyed this." She says, pointed to a red highlight. Urm – should Alexei really be ingesting something that dyes hair like that?

Jim has one of the oddest breweries I've come across. Somehow he's got permission to have a brewery and tasting room at his residential address. The fact that he has a 2.5 acre plot probably helps. But it's still on a very quiet residential street.

Mini Book Series volume XXIV: Tour!

Jim's daughter is pulling beers for a few punters in the tasting room – it's a double garage, really – and when we go to the brewery in the back garden his son Matt is brewing. It's very much a family business. It's a tiny setup - just half a barrel, which is about as small as a commercial brewery can be. I've seen bigger home brew systems.

The plan is for me to hang around the bar to chat and sign books for a few hours. Later, for the event itself, I'll be talking about each of the eight recipes from my book Jim has brewed. I get stuck into his Dark Mild in the meantime.

There's a steady enough stream of punters, quite a few of whom have my book and some of the self-published ones) for me to sign. It's no hardship for me to scribble a few illegible lines and chat a while. I really do enjoy meeting my readers. I hope it's mutual.

I have a fascinating chat with a geologist. "Geology is just as bad as beer for misinformation." He informs me. And there I was thinking it was an objective science. He has some scary stories about exploring abandoned mines. Sounds like a good way of getting yourself killed. Or worse, buried alive.

Steve Nolan and his wife Marissa turn up. He's an English expat who lives on the same street. In fact, that's where I'll be staying tonight as he's kindly offered to put me up. They'll also be providing some of the food – home-made pork pies and sausage rolls – for tonight's event.

Mini Book Series volume XXIV: Tour!

At four everyone is cleared out and the garage door closes. Which is a relief as I was starting to freeze my grillox off. It's unseasonably cold. Bloody arctic vortex. At least it isn't raining. That's what it would usually be doing at this time of year, evidently.

The few books I have left are soon gone. At least I won't be carrying any home with me. I regret not having brought more.

Kickoff is 6 pm. It's a relatively small crowd – the size of the room dictates that – but an enthusiastic and knowledgeable one. Jim has brewed four pairs of beers – two beers in the same of similar styles from different periods – which we sample together.

Scotch Ale
1933 Younger No. 3 Pale
1879 Younger No. 3

Mild Ale
1950 Whitbread Best Ale
1868 Tetley XX

Porter
1886 Barclay Perkins Hhd
1821 Barclay PerkinsTT

Mini Book Series volume XXIV: Tour!

Russian Stout
1941 Barclay Perkins IBS
1924 Barclay Perkins IBS Ex

I explain what the differences are between the beers and why the style changed over time. And lots of other random beer history stuff. It's more tangent than arc this time.

In all, I'm on for around two hours, which is knackering. Even I get fed up of listening to myself talk eventually. I think I've educated and entertained the audience a little.

Jim and his family, me and the Nolans stay on after kicking everyone out for more beer and more talking. After a while I forget how exhausted I am. Maybe because I've finally time to drink some beer.

It ends up being very late. I stay up talking and listening to music with Steve (and drinking Lapghroaig) until after 3 am. By which time I've been up almost 24 hours. I honestly don't know how I do it. I just know it's been a really fun day. One of the best of the trip.

Mini Book Series volume XXIV: Tour!

Fado Irish Pub
801 1st Ave,
Seattle, WA 98104.
Phone: +1 206-264-2700
http://www.fadoirishpub.com/seattle/

Foggy Noggin Brewing
22329 53rd Ave SE,
Bothell, WA 98021.
Phone: +1 425-486-1070
http://www.foggynogginbrewing.com/

Mini Book Series volume XXIV: Tour!

Seattle day four

It's my last bit of a day in the US. I don't feel too bad despite the late-night whisky session. Just as well, as I need to be up reasonably early for breakfast.

This isn't one I want to miss. Steve and Marissa have promised me home-made bacon and sausage, black pudding, crumpets and English tea. Sounds like heaven to me. They're making me feel right at home. It's one of the best meals of my trip.

Dolores would love a garden as large as their 1.25 acres. That's big enough to count as a farm here in Holland. Being that far away from neighbours does make it eerily quiet.

Breakfast done, it's time to go to the airport. Don't want to cut things too fine. It's another beautifully sunny day as Steve drives me along the motorway.

Once I've checked in my bag, toiled through security and snapped up some duty free, I park my arse at the closest bar to my gate. As usual, everyone around is in a chatty mood. I get a double Jack Daniels with a side of Deschutes Porter.

There's the Norwegian bloke going back for his father's funeral. He doesn't look that upset: "He was 93. His passing wasn't exactly unexpected." And a young American woman, who, it turns out, is on the Amsterdam flight, too. She gets a text message from Delta: the flight will be leaving 17 minutes earlier than scheduled. Never had that happen to me before. Just as well I was sitting next to her.

I've had some interesting conversations in airport bars recently. And received some good advice about long flights: take your own food, get to sleep as quickly as possible, have a few drinks before getting on the plane. OK, I didn't need to be told that last one.

I pick up some sushi for the flight. At least I'll have something resembling food to nourish me.

The flight is as exciting as any overnight international flight. Boozed and sushied, I doze reasonably well.

Thankfully my bag appears quickly. I'm soon in a taxi heading for home. After a quick shower and change of clothes, I get the bus to work. What a fun day this will be.

Dungeness Bay Seafood House
Seattle-Tacoma International Airport (SEA),
17801 International Blvd,
Seattle, WA 98158.
Phone: +1 206-787-5388

Mini Book Series volume XXIV: Tour!

V The South

Mini Book Series volume XXIV: Tour!

Houston day one

It all kicks off in Houston. I'm starting there for a very good reason: there's a direct flight from Amsterdam. I've learned my lesson about changing planes. Way too stressful.

Talking of stressful, boarding USA-bound flights at Schiphol has become tense for me. Twice last year I was near as damnit strip searched. It's not a good way to start a journey. To calm my nerves I have a couple of Famous Grouses and a Heineken at the bar adjacent to the gate.

I needn't have worried. They don't say more than two words to me.

Flying across the Atlantic is becoming routine. Not necessarily a pleasure, but not too much of a chore, either. With my extra legroom seat and noise-cancelling headphones, I pass the journey in reasonable comfort, watching crap films to while away the time. And obviously taking full advantage of the free drinks on offer.

Another good reason to fly in via Houston: no ridiculous queues at immigration, unlike some airports. Before I know it, I'm in a taxi bouncing along a freeway lined by endless strip malls. Every single one has a pawn shop. Can't remember seeing many of those when I lived in the US in the 1980's. Maybe I just didn't notice.

I'm stopping downtown. That's what I usually do. Preferably somewhere quite nice. I've picked the Magnolia because I liked the one in Denver so much. Nice old building, comfortable rooms, decent free breakfast. What more do you need?

This is the view from the window:

Mini Book Series volume XXIV: Tour!

The weather is pretty crap. Wet, humid and surprisingly warm. I've deliberately come in the spring, knowing what southern summer weather is like.

I've a couple of hours to get my head straightened before meeting Noel Hart at 4 PM. He's helped organise tomorrow with his home brew club the Foam Rangers (great name).

We're headed for the Flying Saucer, a beer pub handily situated just a couple of blocks from my hotel. It's a fairly cavernous place, with a high ceiling and an enormous beer list. Loads of US beers, but equally plenty of European imports. Not that I'm going to bother with any of the latter. Just as I usually avoid American beers in Europe. Unsurprisingly, it being Friday, it's pretty boisterous inside.

We chat and drink. A few other people turn up. Until I hit a wall at about 9 pm. I think that's when it was. I didn't do that badly, when you consider it was 4 am for me. And I'd been up over 20 hours.

It's pissing it down when I leave. I wake up in bed at 1 am, fully clothed, TV on. Must have dropped off while watching something.

Mini Book Series volume XXIV: Tour!

I sleep deeply well past dawn.

Foam Rangers and De Falco's tomorrow.

The Flying Saucer
705 Main St
Houston, TX 77002
http://www.beerknurd.com/stores/houston/

Mini Book Series volume XXIV: Tour!

Houston day two

I'm still a bit knacked, even after a good long sleep. So after stuffing scrambled eggs and bacon down my throat I head back upstairs for a bit of a lie down.

Just as well I'm in no rush. Noel Hart is picking me up at midday to drive me out to DeFalco's, the home brew shop where I'm having an event. It's always fun watching random US TV.

I particularly enjoy the adverts for prescription drugs. Where they say how miraculous it is then quickly rattle through a list of side effects, including such minor things as stroke, heart attack or death. They always make me smile.

When I get to DeFalco's I realise something: all the strip malls in Houston are painted the same sand colour.

The event is in a back room. I say event, it's really just me chatting about beer and trying to sell books. That's becoming the story of my life. They've brewed up some recipes from the book so I do get to drink beer, too. There's a 19th-century Whitbread X - always love

Mini Book Series volume XXIV: Tour!

those old Mild recipes. If only because they're nothing like Mild as it's now understood.

A nice Scottish IPA is great. And 1885 Younger XP certainly plugs that hole in my dyke. It's another good style for confusing the unwary, Scottish IPA. The 1900 Grätzer proves once again what a cracking - and seriously neglected - style it is.

I'm given a rather cool Foam Rangers badge, the shape and size of a sheriff's badge. Thanks.

It's a pretty relaxed couple of hours. But my belly is calling. I'm taken to The Hay Merchant, a beer bar crammed with what mostly looked like young things. It's hard to tell when the lights are low and you're as old as me.

Maybe you can check on the photo:

Mini Book Series volume XXIV: Tour!

Hard to tell when everyone has their back turned, isn't it?

Let's try with this one. Bit blurry, but at least a few are facing the right way:

Fairly young crowd. Look at those beards.

I get a tour of the cellar. As you can see, they have one or two draught beers:

I leave pretty early. Or rather I'm driven back fairly early hen I start nodding off and dribbling down my shirt. Still not totally at home in this time zone. Couldn't possibly be anything to do with drinking beer for hours on end.

Tomorrow it's my luxury flight to glamourous Birmingham, Alabama. Need to be at my freshest.

Defalco's Homebrew
9223 Stella link Rd.
Houston, TX 77025
http://www.defalcos.com/

Mini Book Series volume XXIV: Tour!

The Hay Merchant
1100 Westheimer Rd
Houston, TX 77006.
http://www.haymerchant.com/

Mini Book Series volume XXIV: Tour!

Birmingham day one

The Alabama, not West Midlands one. I'm sure you're aware of that, but just making sure.

I have to be up reasonably early as my flight is just after 10 AM. And I've a couple of bags to check in. After loading up of eggs and bacon, I check out and get a cab.

Rattling around in the back, I notice a disconcerting sign: "Concealed weapons prohibited". Does that mean unconcealed weapons are OK? It must, otherwise surely it would just say "Weapons prohibited".

I've splashed out on a first class ticket, which means I get two free checkin bags. May as well take advantage. I've also got the TSA express thing, which means I can leave on some of my clothing during the security check. I had this last time I was in the US, too. No idea why, but I'm not complaining.

George Bush International is a funny place. A big, international airport, but few eat/drink/shop opportunities. Very odd. Most airports nowadays are like shopping centres with an auxiliary transport function.

I'm looking for a bar. There's a breakfasty type place, but, significantly, the seats at the bar are all tilted forward. Looks like it isn't open yet. I eventually find somewhere more bar-like, only to be told they can't serve me a beer yet. This is as bad as Toronto airport. Even in Britain you can get a beer airside at 8 AM. I have a coffee instead.

Having a first class ticket, I can board early. I've got seat 1A, another perk of flying first class. It's conveniently close to the galley. Something that's very handy during the flight. Dead easy for me to ask for another whisky, which I do several times during the flight.

I'm collected at the airport by Nick Hudson, a member of the homebrewing club the Carboy Junkies.

"Do you want to go straight to your hotel or have a beer first?"

It's a principle of mine never to turn down a beer. Ever. We head for Paramount, which is downtown, not far from my hotel.

It's one of those odd places that combines beer, food and old arcade games. We order a very good hamburger and I shovel down a few beers.

As you can see, it's very light inside. I quite like the place.

Mini Book Series volume XXIV: Tour!

I've just about time to check in before it's time to head over to Cahaba Brewing, the location of today's event.

With a 3.5 barrel brewhouse, they're at the small end of production breweries. It looks like they've still plenty of room to expand. The brewing revival is very recent here, partly due to crazy alcohol laws, like a ceiling on ABV. And a ban on home brewing. That's all by way of explanation of the fact that, although Cahaba was only founded in 2011, they're one of Alabama's older breweries.

The tap room is smack bang in the brewery. Which I'd find disconcerting were I a brewer. But I've seen it more often in newer breweries, for example in Seattle.

It a simple, unpretentious place:

Mini Book Series volume XXIV: Tour!

Carboy Junkies have set up a small bar, serving six historic beers:

- 1855 Barclay Perkins EI Porter
- 1879 Younger No. 3
- 1914 Fullers AK
- 1924 Barclay Perkins RNS "Royal Navy" Stout
- 1952 Lees Best Mild
- 1955 Whitbread Double Brown Ale

I'd like to say, all beers from my book. But only the Younger's No. 3 is. Double Brown was in, but got cut for space reasons. It's a good spread of styles, with only a Pale Ale and a Strong Ale missing.

I chat merrily with club members about all things beer history and enjoy the occasional beer. That Lees Mild recipe is a cracker. Been very popular with home brewers. Why didn't I include it in the book? I remember: it's Kristen's recipe.

Someone presses a badge into my hand. At first I think it's a club badge, like the one I was given in Houston. Then I see the anchor and the words "Barclay Perkins". It was

Mini Book Series volume XXIV: Tour!

given to William Thomas Jackson to celebrate 21 years' service. Wow. I don't know what to say. It's a wonderful gift.

One of the club members I chat with is Scotsman Stuart Carter. He's taking me on a brewery crawl tomorrow. Can't wait.

Paramount
200 20th St N,
Birmingham, AL 35203
info@paramountbirmingham.com
http://www.paramountbirmingham.com/

Cahaba Brewing Company
2616 3rd Ave S,
Birmingham, Alabama 35233
http://www.cahababrewing.com/

Mini Book Series volume XXIV: Tour!

Birmingham day two

I'm stopping in quite a nice hotel downtown, Hampton Inn & Suites-Downtown-Tutwiler. But the free breakfast buffet has paper plates and plastic cutlery. I've come across this a few times in the US. It looks really, really crap.

Stuart Carter picks me up after brekkie with his toddler son, Jamie. We head off on a slow ramble around Birmingham's beery spots.

On the way to our first stop, Stuart explains the geography of Birmingham. Railway tracks run approximately East to West, slicing the town in two. With the Southside to the South and the Northside to the East. (Little pop culture reference there.) Most of the breweries are in the Southside, which makes sense as it's the more industrial half of the city.

We start at Hop City, a bottle shop and growler filling station. It's quite an impressive selection, including lots of beer from the UK and the rest of Europe. Even better, all those draught taps mean we can enjoy a glass of beer while we watch it piss down with rain outside. The weather continues to be dreadful.

Mini Book Series volume XXIV: Tour!

Our second stop is North of the tracks. It's still raining when we get there and I rush inside quickly to avoid a right soaking. You find some odd combinations in the US. Bottle & Bone is certainly one: restaurant, butcher and bottle shop. And I mean a proper butcher that makes its own bacon and sausages. There's draught beer, too. A little Spartan, but the meat looks dead, dead good. A shame it isn't quite time for lunch yet.

Back over the tracks again, the rain has finally stopped for a while as we pull up outside Avondale Brewing. A brewery Stuart tells me has been pivotal in revitalising what had been a very run-down part of town. I'm surprised to spot a room full of open fermenters as we enter. For their sour beers, Stuart tells me.

We chat to a bearded (aren't they all) brewer a little but he's very busy. The brewing crew is leaving for the CBC tomorrow and they have lots to finish up. I'm intrigued by one of their beer names: Brothel Brown. It seems the building used to house a seedy bar with a house of ill repute upstairs.

Mini Book Series volume XXIV: Tour!

Remaining Southside, Trim Tab, another brewery, is next on the list. Quite a barn of a place is some sort of former workshop. Stuart recommends their ESB, but there's only the very bottom of a keg left. The brewer squeezes a little out. It's past its best but still nice. (Excuse the over-technical beer descriptions. I've left my thesaurus at home.)

We decant to the taproom, where we can sample cask. Always my first choice, if I believe it's been looked after. It's an Old Ale, dark and full. It's another space untouched by luxury. Like the Lucha libre-themed art.

Eating. I find it's a good idea to indulge in it a couple of times a day. Barbecue seems a good idea. We try Saw's Soul Kitchen, just a few doors away. But it's packed. Waiting in a small, crowded place for an indeterminate time with a toddler doesn't seem a great idea.

Mini Book Series volume XXIV: Tour!

Stuart suggests Jim 'N Nick's. I'm easy. Anything that makes life simple. The cheese biscuits are never-ending and they sell beer. I'm sold. We chomp down some barbecue while Jamie charms the women in next booth. Gets much harder when you get older, champ, charming the ladies.

The rain is now gone, though the streets are drenched and every step challenges to engulf my shoes in red mud. We head for the final brewery in the set of four Birmingham breweries, Good People. I've already tried their beer.

The brewery is cavernous, industrial and opposite Regions Field, home of Birmingham Barons baseball team. There seems to be something going on there as part of the road is closed and people are milling about inside.

Stuart recommends Snake Handler IPA. Seems they shift as much as they can brew of it. I settle for an alternative IPA. But luckily once I've downed that, the Snake Handler IPA is back. And very nice it is, too, in a alcoholy way. It's a sessionable 9.3%.

Mini Book Series volume XXIV: Tour!

We finish in in J. Clyde, an Englishy-style pub that has cask beer. The Trim Tab Old Ale. It's still raining.

I won't tell you the horrors of trying to find somewhere to eat later. Let's just say the Paramount was closed and I ate in my hotel.

Avondale Brewing
201 41st St S,
Birmingham, AL 35222
http://avondalebrewing.com/

Trim Tab Brewing
2721 5th Ave S,
Birmingham, AL 35233
http://trimtabbrewing.com/

Mini Book Series volume XXIV: Tour!

Jim 'N Nick's Bar-B-Q
1908 11th Ave S,
Birmingham, AL 35205.

Good People Brewing Company
114 14th St S,
Birmingham, AL 35233,
http://www.goodpeoplebrewing.com/

The J. Clyde
1312 Cobb Ln,
Birmingham, AL 35205
http://jclyde.com/

Mini Book Series volume XXIV: Tour!

Atlanta day one

This is going to be a strange day. I'm travelling to Atlanta, but my train doesn't leave until 2:30 PM. Leaving me quite a few hours to kill in downtown Birmingham.

At first I consider strangling it at Paramount. Then I realise that they don't open until 4 PM. Damn. Until I recall somewhere else I stumbled on while researching the trip: Rogue Tavern. It's not too far away and seems to have a decent choice of beer. I leave my luggage at the hotel and head off.

On the way over it becomes clear that the regeneration of downtown Birmingham is far from over. Away from the shiny new office blocks there are plenty of dead buildings and empty lots. Not the cheeriest of sights. Not raining.

Though I'm starting to wish it was. In the sun it feels effing hot. And just as humid as when it was raining.

At last I've found a bar downtown that's open. Away from the gleaming skyscrapers, it's a bit rundown. I leave my change with a polite gentleman down on his luck.

Mini Book Series volume XXIV: Tour!

This is where I used to waste my breath employing those wordy things to describe stuff. Barn, lunching office workers, look at the photos:

It's not yet noon, but the waitress asks: "Are you eating."

"Later. I need to work up an appetite."

A good place to start seems:

Good People Snake Handler

A very popular beer, according to Stuart. And highly sessionable at just 10% ABV. (I've made that joke before, haven't I?) It's a pretty amber colour, with only the slightest haze. [Beer description warning] The aroma is citrus, with maybe a hint of peach. In the mouth there's a load more fruit, malt hiding somewhere behind the settee, afraid to come out. Not stupidly bitter, as seems to be the trend.

Not so sure a double – or is it triple? – IPA is the most sensible beer to kick off with. But

Mini Book Series volume XXIV: Tour!

I've only a couple of hours before getting on the train. For 5 hours, I'll be booze-free. Best get tanked up now.

Trying to stick with Alabama beers, I've ordered:

Back Forty Truck Stop

Billed as an English Brown Ale, it's 6% ABV. Guess it's a Northern Brown, then. The colour is deep amber, just about nudging up to fully fledged brown. Something a bit weird tasting about it. That funny straw flavour Bass XXXX Mild from Taddy used to have.

Don't want to pig out so soon after breakfast. Southern Brisket Sandwich it is. Just what I needed. Not stupidly huge. Tasty and served with a few chips.

I get another Snake Handler. Liked me that stuff. It is surprisingly drinkable – much more so than the Brown Ale.

None of the lunching office people are drinking beer. Only me. But I'm on holiday. And

Mini Book Series volume XXIV: Tour!

Americans don't drink during work hours. Mostly.

Just as well this is a short session. Snake Handler is going down way too easy.

Not raining when I leave – whahay!

After picking up my bags, I get a cab to the train station. It's not far, but my luggage weighs a ton. It's all those books. The station is a shockingly small affair, a good bit smaller than Newark North Gate, which only caters for 35,000 inhabitants. It brings home how marginal train travel is in much of the US.

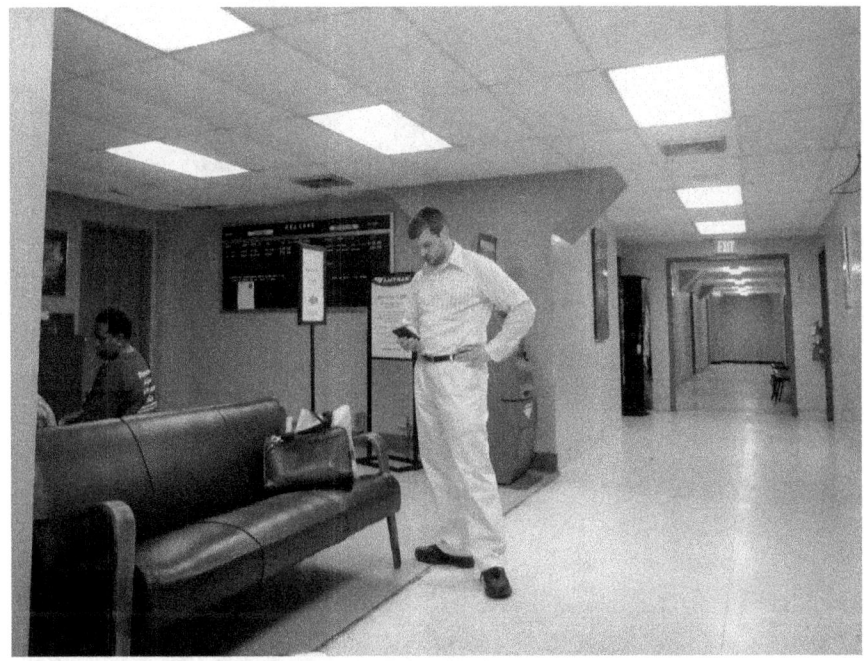

The train is a bog-standard Amtrak affair. The type with the very narrow windows. Thousands of these coaches must have been built. They're getting a bit long in the tooth, but are comfortable enough and quite spacious.

On the way out of town we run alongside a dead steel works. It's just like being back in the north of England.

Mini Book Series volume XXIV: Tour!

We pass this, which I think will impress Andrew:

Mini Book Series volume XXIV: Tour!

I while away the journey finally looking at the TV progs Dolores has put on my netbook. Though it's a bastard keeping the plug in the socket. Again. Had the same thing on the Vancouver – Seattle train.

The Amtrak station in Atlanta is small and bizarrely far from downtown. I manage to miss Crawford Moran, who's hosting me tonight. He waits in the baggage hall. But I had no checked in bags.

I take a cab to my downtown hotel. The location is great. Something I hadn't been able to work out from looking at maps. The centre of a US city can be strangely elusive on maps.

I check in. Brilliant. I've a suite. With a wonderful view. Shame I have to jump in a taxi almost straight away. No time to enjoy the luxury. I'm almost already late for the 9 PM event at 5 Seasons Westside.

My taxi driver has the radio tuned to a lunatic right-wing shock jock. Though he doesn't seem impressed. "This guy is crazy." Why are you listening to him, then?

I'm pleased to find a few people assembled to greet and bullshit with inside. It's quite late

Mini Book Series volume XXIV: Tour!

and a school night. Everyone is very nice.

Crawford has brewed 1853 Younger XP. I love this beer. A style nazi confusing hoppy Scottish beer. Brilliantly, he's serving haggis to accompany it. Dead cool.

Before taking me home, Crawford gives me a tour of the brewery in the basement. I'm surprised at its size. And the quality of the brickwork on the back wall. Geeking out about bonds – that's even rarer than geeking out about beer.

I sleep the just sleep of the moderately intoxicated with a bottle of water within reach.

Rogue Tavern
2312 2nd Ave N,
Birmingham, AL 35203
http://www.roguetavern.com/

Mini Book Series volume XXIV: Tour!

5 Seasons Westside
1000 Marietta St NW #204,
Atlanta, GA 30318
http://www.5seasonsbrewing.com/

Mini Book Series volume XXIV: Tour!

Atlanta day two

Good news is that breakfast is included in the room price. Bad news is that it's another disposable plate/cutlery/cups affair. Weird in quite a nice hotel where I have a suite.

I go back to my room for a lie down after I've eaten. No rush today. My event isn't until the evening.

Around noon I take a wander down the main drag. I hadn't realized just how downtown I was. American cities can be hard to work out from maps. Where exactly is the city centre? It's not always easy to spot.

I'm vaguely headed towards Max Lager's brewery. Though I'm not totally committed to reaching it. It's a bit of a walk and I'm a lazy git.

Atlanta isn't like I expected. Downtown is far livelier than Birmingham. It reminds me a bit of Manhattan. Tall buildings, lots of people milling about. Sort of like a city. No half wrecked buildings, either. I quite like the place. They've even got trams.

I spot an Irish pub, walk past, than go back and peer through the window. Looks like they have a few beers as well as the usual Guinness and Kilkenny crap. And, as I used to tell the kids, it is unlucky to walk past a pub that's open.

Mini Book Series volume XXIV: Tour!

I take a seat at the bar, as I usually do when I'm alone. What to try first? Something local. I opt for

Sweetwater Imperial Stout
It's black as night on the dark side of the moon. Nice looking head. Imperial Stout – the perfect lunchtime drink. Bit odd getting it in a Newkie Brown glass. A pleasant enough balance of citrus and roast. Not too crazy and pretty drinkable.

US pricing structures are weird. My 9% Imperial Stout costs the same as 5% Guinness Blonde, $7. What a strange place the US is. No wonder session beer has such a hard time.

Time for another beer.

Sweetwater PA
Not too murky, but little head. Bit bland, if I'm honest. Little aroma, bit of bitterness, but not much going on. Won't be having another.

They have homemade salt and vinegar crisps on the menu. I need to eat something, but not too much as breakfast wasn't long ago. I just get a starter, Devils on Horseback. It fills my food hole perfectly.

Just noticed that they have both Smithwicks and Kilkenny. Aren't they the same beer?

I stray outside Georgia for my next beer

Goose Island IPA
Crystal clear, thin head. Not much aroma again. But some citrus peel in the gob.

On the way to the bog I notice a Tetley pub sign. That's not very Irish, is it? Though some of the best Irish pubs in Leeds were Tetley houses.

Brings a tear to my eye. The house style of Tetley's houses from the 1970's. So many memories of Leeds flood back like the beer over a glass the economiser way. Black Dog, Cardigan Arms, Rising Sun. Sheepscar, Roscoe, Regent, Brassmoulders Arms, Garden Gate and many other wonderful Tetley's pubs, where the Mild was spot on pint after pint.

We won't see those days again.

Mini Book Series volume XXIV: Tour!

I don't stay too late. This evening's event is at 6 PM. And it's miles out in Acworth.

My taxi takes quite a while to turn up. When we hit the motorway, I realise that it's rush hour. We aren't going as fast as I'd hoped, due to the heavy traffic. I'm supposed to be meeting, who's organizing the event, at 5 PM in Freight Kitchen & Tap in Woodstock for a bite to eat. I'm not going to make it. Not even vaguely.

By the time the taxi pulls up there, it's almost 6 PM. I bump into David, who's just about to leave, in the parking lot. No time to eat, so we head directly to Dogwood Growlers, site of the event.

I'm not sure what they have planned. Seems they want me to do some talking. No problem. I do half an hour or so on historic beer. I've spoken on the topic so often that I can do it in my sleep[7]. Come to think of it I do sometimes in my dreams. I get some good questions from the audience. That always livens things up.

After drinking some beer and flogging a few books, we go for a bite to eat. When it starts getting late, I get a limo back to my hotel. It's quite late. And I need to be up fairly early. I've a Greyhound bus to catch. Riding a Greyhound is always an . . . experience, let's just say that.

Max Lager's Wood-Fired Grill & Brewery
320 Peachtree St NE
Atlanta, GA 30308

Meehan's Public House
200 Peachtree St NE
Atlanta, GA 30303
http://www.meehansdowntown.com/

Freight Kitchen & Tap
251 E Main St
Woodstock, GA 30188
http://www.freightkitchen.com/

---

[7] I do according to Dolores.

Mini Book Series volume XXIV: Tour!

Asheville day one

My Greyhound is quite early, 9:15. After the long wait for a taxi yesterday, I'm not taking any chances and get up in plenty of time.

After a quick breakfast, I check out and ask them to call me a cab. Then the lady on the desk suggests I use the hotel shuttle and cancels my cab.

I'm not going far and would happily have walked to the Greyhound station, were it not for my luggage. But I'm shocked at how short a distance the first person off the bus travels. It's really just the other side of the street. It can't be more than 20 metres from the hotel entrance. The second off doesn't go much further. And neither is carrying anything. Lazy gits.

The small waiting room at the station is packed and chaotic. It's not exactly the cream of American society. I feel right at home. A security guard has a flaming argument with a passenger for no apparent reason. This is great. Free entertainment to while away my waiting time.

The bus is late. When it arrives there's a mad scramble to get on and grab seats. I didn't realise that you have to check in bags you want to put in the baggage compartment. So I have to squeeze my trolley bag in next to me. Not much room left for my legs. It's not the most comfortable position. I console myself with the thought that it's only for three and a half hours.

Once outside the city, the small town strip malls we pass have most of their signs in Spanish. How odd. The bus stops are around the back of a petrol stations in dismal malls. Other than Atlanta, this service doesn't seem to venture into town centres.

As we approach South Carolina, billboards advertising Crazy Joe's fireworks become more frequent. I guess the laws on fireworks are more relaxed in South Carolina than in Georgia.

My destination is Greenville, where Mike Karnowski is picking me up and driving me to Asheville. I'm relieved to see that he's there waiting for me. We met last year in Chicago,

Mini Book Series volume XXIV: Tour!

of all places. Even better, he's brought a sandwich and some beer for me. A Grodziskie, which is rather nice. Smoky and hoppy, as it should be.

On the way we chat about brewer, but also music. In common with many brewers, he also has a passion for music. I mention my dream of forming a garage punk band with Dann Paquette and Mitch Steel. All we need is a drummer. Sadly, Mike's another guitarist.

We pick up his other half, Gabe, from their home and head straight to the Green Man, where Mike's a brewer. Though not for much longer. He tells me he's just handed in his notice. He's starting his own brewery in a former fire station. Yet another brewery in Asheville. The place is full of them.

Mike gives me a quick tour of the brewery. I'm dead impressed by the number of my books he has in his office. I have a feeling that a large percentage of my self-published books have found a home in brewing rooms around the world.

After a quick beer in Green Man, we head off on a quick brewery crawl of the South Slope. First stop is Burial Brewing, which has a weird gothic vibe. The tap room isn't open yet, but as the bearded brewers know Mike, they let us in.

Mini Book Series volume XXIV: Tour!

It's a pretty small industrial unit, with the brewing kit at the rear and a small tap room at the front. This seems to be a pretty common layout in the more recent breweries. The tap room isn't really separated from the brewing part of the premises.

Hi-Wire is next. A little further up the hill. Not really used to hills after so many years living in Holland. Walking them up them isn't my favourite pastime. They're just about opening so we get a beer. They've six of their own plus 3 guests on tap. Again, the drinking and serving area is wedged between the brewing equipment.

Mini Book Series volume XXIV: Tour!

That weird. They've got a Newcastle flag next to an Arsenal one. Don't they realise over here that you're supposed to hate Arsenal?

We head back down the hill to our next stop, Funkatorium. It's the wild beer offshoot of one of the city centre's larger breweries, Wicked Weed. This feels a slicker operation, with a stronger division between brewing and drinking. At the rear, there's an impressive stack of wooden barrels and even a foeder. Complete with signs telling you not to touch them.

If I had a brewery, I'd keep any bugs well away from my main brewery. Preferably in another state or, better still, on another continent. Too much scope for things going horribly wrong. You're pretty much buggered once Brettanomyces takes hold. That stuff is almost impossible to kill.

They sell a mix of sour and non-sour beers. I go for one of the former. Only sour of the trip so far.

We cross the road to Twin Leaf, which is directly opposite. Here the brewing kit is separated from the drinking area by a low wall. Everything is still in one room, but there's a definite division of space going on.

We don't have far to walk to our next stop. Catawba Brewing is just a few doors away. The company has been around since the 1990's and this is their third location. Their main brewery is on the southern edge of town.

This time it's just a rope between the seating and brewing areas. The latter being partly stacked with wooden barrels. When did I last visit a brewery without wooden barrels ageing something? I can't remember. Everyone is doing it nowadays.

I mention that Lexie had requested sour sweets and they lead me to Mast, an old-fashioned general store on the main drag. I've more than enough choice of retro sweets.

Our final port of call is Wicked Weed, by far the slickest operation of the day. Their taproom is large and stylish. It reminds me of a smaller version of Stone's bar in Escondido. We go downstairs, which is a little rougher around the edges and shares the space with the brewing kit.

Mini Book Series volume XXIV: Tour!

All I can say about Asheville is wow. I've never been anywhere – not even in Franconia – with so many breweries in such a small area. Everywhere we've been is within 500 metres of Green Man. Most within 100 metres.

I'm dropped at my hotel to check in, but they pick me up again later. We're off to a homebrew club meeting. Bizarrely, it's in a German restaurant, the Black Forest. Mike takes along some of his Grodziskie and I stand up and talk a little about the style. I get a few laughs, which is always a good sign. And I sell a few books, which is even better.

While I'm having a nightcap in the hotel bar, I get talking to a couple sat next to me at the bar. I tell them why I'm in town – pushing my book – and they seem quite interested. I manage to sell them a copy.

It's been a good day.

Green Man
27 Buxton Ave
Asheville, NC 28801
http://www.greenmanbrewery.com/

Burial Beer Co.
40 Collier Ave
Asheville, NC 28801
http://www.burialbeer.com/

Hi-Wire Brewing
197 Hilliard Ave
Asheville, NC 28801
http://hiwirebrewing.com/

Funkatorium
145 Coxe Ave
Asheville, NC 28801

Twin Leaf Brewery
144 Coxe Ave
Asheville, NC 28801
http://www.twinleafbrewery.com/

Catawba Brewing Company
32 Banks Ave #105
Asheville, NC 28801
http://catawbabrewingco.com

Wicked Weed Brewing
91 Biltmore Ave
Asheville, NC 28801
http://www.wickedweedbrewing.com/

Black Forest Restaurant
2155 Hendersonville Rd
Arden, NC 28704
http://www.blackforestasheville.com

Mini Book Series volume XXIV: Tour!

Asheville day two

I forgot to ask yesterday if breakfast is included. I realise my mistake when I trundle up to reception to ask for a cab. "Buffet breakfast included". Oh well. Good for my waistline.

I hadn't realised while being ferried around by Gabe (she was dedicated driver while Mike and I indulged) how far Fletcher is from Asheville. It's a fair old drive on the motorway. Why am I staying all the way out here? Because my hotel is where the shuttle bus to Charlotte airport picks up. I need to get the bus at 6 AM. Staying at the hotel saves me having to get up before I go to bed and a nerve-jangling crosstown dash.

Now there's an indication this is a small town. My taxi driver conscientiously fills in all the fields in my receipt. Never had that happen before. They usually just give you a blank form.

I've come to Green Man to drop off books for this evening. Hopefully, I won't have to take many back to my hotel.

Mini Book Series volume XXIV: Tour!

My plan? To troll around some more breweries. There are a few I didn't get to yesterday. The ones at the top of the hill. Time to sort that out.

Food. It's a recurring theme with my stomach. Can't stop pestering me about it. To escape from its endless nagging, I ball up with the place most likely to shut it up: Wicked Weed. It's up the hill. But I've no choice.

Considering the early hour – it's not yet noon – there's a decent crowd in already. But still a seat at the bar for me. "Give me the food menu, but I'll order later. I need to work up an appetite first." And torture my effing gut a bit.

Let's get some beer.

Lil Heresy Brown Ale 5.2%

Nice Mahogany colour, little head. Quite roasty. Is that brown malt? I shouldn't guess about ingredients. It only makes you look like a prat. Not a lot of hop character, but I can live with that. Makes for a nice change of pace.

Mini Book Series volume XXIV: Tour!

I really like Asheville. Cool, cool town with friendly people. And, being quite high up, it isn't too effing hot. Nor humid.

Should I tell the barman there's no evidence Henry VIII ever said the phrase "wicked and pernicious weed"? Maybe I'll keep that for this evening. After I explain what Ale and Beer meant.

I'm still recovering from the walk up that hill. A wimp, I know.

Time for another beer.

English Bitter 4.8%

Very pale yellow, little head. Nice earthy Goldings aroma (see above on the dangers of guessing ingredients). Bit light on malt character.

Not too thrilled by that. Probably would have impressed more on cask.

More beer. Bit light on the casual observations of my fellow boozers today. Sorry. Other things on my mind. Like where's my next beer.

Don't Tread on Maize

Crazy name, crazy beer. American Pale Ale with flaked maize. Sounds like an AK. Very pale amber. Oddly, it's darker than the English Bitter. (Someone needs to lay down a framework of precise style definitions to prevent this sort of confusion.) Quite bitter, without being hugely aromatic. There's some citrus zest bitterness at the back end. A pleasant enough beer. Sidles down my throat supply enough.

Time to up the octanes.

Conquistador 9.1% ABV
[That's enough beer snaps. Instead the scene to my right.]

Mezcal, smoked malt, lime juice and grapefruit zest. Happening disaster to a? I expected something dark. Smells like lime-flavoured antiseptic. Interesting. Surprisingly, in a good way. Though not as nice as the smell of mashing wafting up from the brewery downstairs. Not the car crash you might have expected from the ingredients.

Mini Book Series volume XXIV: Tour!

My bison burger has arrived:

Mini Book Series volume XXIV: Tour!

Very nice it is. As it's my first (and possibly only) meal of the day, I eat all the chips. There aren't that many.

Here's the weed guy at the end of the room:

My stomach is now moaning about the quantity of beer coming its way. Mithering twat. It should see what's coming. I wonder if Henry ever had this sort of trouble?

More Asheville brewery crawling coming up.

Green Man
27 Buxton Ave
Asheville, NC 28801
http://www.greenmanbrewery.com/

Wicked Weed Brewing
91 Biltmore Ave
Asheville, NC 28801
http://www.wickedweedbrewing.com/

Mini Book Series volume XXIV: Tour!

Mini Book Series volume XXIV: Tour!

Asheville day two (part two)

I missed some of the breweries yesterday. So I don't linger too long in Wicked Weed. My next stop is over the other side of the hill that forms the centre of town.

Lexington Avenue Brewing is less industrial than most of the other breweries I've visited in town, with the exception of Wicked Weed. I take a seat at the bar, as usual. What to drink? Think I'll try

Three Threads Porter
Beer myths seem a recurring theme today. Very dark brown, but not black. "English-style Brown Porter" it's called. Strange, as that's a non-existent style. Not roasty enough. And no brown malt in the grist, so not really an English Porter.

As I mentioned, it's slicker than most of the other breweries. The brewing kit is behind glass at the rear rather than being up close and personal

Mini Book Series volume XXIV: Tour!

At least the beer is cheap: $3.75 for a US pint of 5.1% Porter.

I get chatting to a young couple sitting next to me at the bar. They're from New Hampshire but are looking to move to the South. Asheville, Nashville or Charlotte. Interesting choices. Asheville is a charming place set amongst wooded hills. But it would be too small for me. And too far from anywhere else. A hippy island in southern sea. As Mike told me yesterday: "You can't swing a brewer without hitting a yoga teacher."

Time for another beer

Hop Burst IPA
Quite nice. Bitter, orange-peely. You can tell I'm getting tired. The beer descriptions are getting curter.

Time for one final brewery before returning to Green Man for my talk. I have a bit of trouble finding One World Brewing, despite having map of the town's breweries. It's down a short alley, through an unmarked door. Bit like a speakeasy.

Dolores wouldn't be keen. She doesn't like subterranean places. It does seem an odd spot for a brewery. I'm glad the fermenters are in a sealed room. Wouldn't want to be killed by CO2.

Inner Thigh IPA 6.5% ABV
Pretty damn murky. Quite malty – I've have suspected malt extract if I couldn't see a mash tun over against the wall. A small one, admittedly. I've seen home brew systems that were as large. Looks about 1 US barrel.

Some people come in that I recognise from earlier. I'm clearly not the only one on a brewery crawl.

Time to be getting to Green Man. But when I get outside it's pissing it down with rain. And I've no coat with me. I have another beer, but it's still pissing it down. No choice but to bite the bullet. I can't miss my own talk. I try to take what cover I can, but still get pretty wet.

My shirt is so wet, I'm given a Green Man hoody to wear.

There's a decent crowd. I do my just saying what comes into my head thing for an hour

Mini Book Series volume XXIV: Tour!

or so. It's a knowledgeable audience and I get some decent questions. Always nice to wander off into uncharted territory. Stops me getting bored with telling the same stories over and again.

I don't stay out late. I've an early start tomorrow. A very early start. I'm catching the shuttle bus to Charlotte at 6 AM.

Lexington Avenue Brewery
39 N Lexington Ave,
Asheville, NC 28801.
Tel: +1 828-252-0212
http://www.lexavebrew.com/

One World Brewing
10 Patton Ave,
Asheville, NC 28801.
Tel: +1 828-785-5580
http://www.oneworldbrewing.com/

Houston final day

I'm up early. Very early. I've arranged a wakeup call for 5 AM. I'm too early for breakfast, which kicks off at six.

I hope the shuttle bus company got my booking OK. I haven't had a confirmation. Not booking until yesterday was a bit stupid of me. I knew I'd be taking it weeks ago. Still, I'm sure everything will be fine.

I stand outside with my bags 15 minutes early, at quarter to six. It's pretty quiet, though there are a couple of people smoking.

I start getting worried at 6:05. By 6:15 I'm shitting serious building material. Looks like I may have to take a taxi. Why didn't I book the stupid shuttle earlier? It's quite a distance to Charlotte so a taxi will be expensive. But I have to get to Charlotte on time. If I miss my flight, there isn't another to Houston until tomorrow.

At 6:30 I admit that the bus isn't coming. And go back inside to arrange a taxi. The woman behind the desk rings around the local taxi firms. None can do the 120-mile ride in the morning. If they could, it would cost $280.

Excrement Alley, propelling instrument-free is where I am. Then the woman on the desk says, "Wait 15 minutes and I'll take you." What a relief. My kecks were only a few minutes away from a good browning. (Not such a disaster, as I have a supply of trollies and kecks, just no more transport possibilities.)

Now I do have time for a quick brekkie. Though my stomach is churning so much I've zero appetite.

At the end of her night shift, she'll spend four hours driving a total stranger to the airport and then back home. I'm not sure I'd do it.

We drive through some very rural – and scenic – bits of North Carolina. But I can't really pay the scenery much attention. I'm still worried about making it to the airport on time. Luckily, the traffic is light – it is Saturday morning, after all.

Of course, I give the kind lady petrol money and a good wadge of dosh, but she hadn't asked for anything. She's really saved me. As my flight back to Amsterdam is tomorrow, I could quite easily have missed that, too.

Restores your faith in humanity.

Checking in, I'm surprised to see that I've got two free checkin bags. I'm flying Southwest, which is a cheapo carrier. They don't even have assigned seats. I'm not complaining. Saves me carrying all my junk around the airport.

Mini Book Series volume XXIV: Tour!

I've time for a couple of drinks airside. I have a few Knob Creeks. Purely to settle my nerves, you understand. I'm still feeling a bit shaky from all the worry.

On the ground in Houston, it's another long, bouncy-castle ride past endless sand-coloured strip malls to my hotel. I'm in the Magnolia again. A really nice hotel and right in the centre of town. Plus there's the Flying Saucer just around the corner.

Which is where I head after dumping my bags and doing a little light shopping. It's quite full, but I find a spot at the bar. Mini-skirted waitresses dance around the room, ferrying glasses of delight to all corners.

It's only 14:45, but I'm knacked. Up at five then a stack of stress. I order a beer from one of the serving lasses.

Mini Book Series volume XXIV: Tour!

Martin House Cellarman's IPA
Not much of a cellarman, I think, as it's murky as hell. Not hugely aromatic, but pretty bitter. Not sure the murk is helping the flavour.

Next I try:

Saint Arnold Icon Blue
This is a better-looking beer: dark amber, pretty clear, nice fluffy head. Classic grapefruit-driven IPA. Really nice and aromatic, lots of citrus all the way through. Quite nice.

Bearded men and tattooed ladies. At least you can shave off a beard when it goes out of fashion. Here it's not arm but leg tattoos. Weird and incredibly unsexy. I need more beer.

(512) Pecan Porter
How more southern can you get? I suppose it could have a shotgun in it, too. Pretty black. Totally opaque. Not much head. Roasted malt aroma. Liquorice. Like liquid ink. Hang on, ink is liquid. At least until it dries. Like ink, but tastier. Like old school Porter/Stout – loads of black malt (or something similar).

I've hit a wall again. Not literally, obviously. I order some food – a pork stew. When it comes, it doesn't look like I expected. It's in a shallow frying pan and covered in melted cheese. Accompanied by flour tortillas. Pretty nice. I needed more food. A light breakfast is all I've eaten today.

Mini Book Series volume XXIV: Tour!

A final beer before I return to my hotel for a lie down.

Martin House Mind on my Money 9.2% ABV
Another murky one. Seems a thing with Martin House. Grapefruit and caramel. Actually some malt in this one.

After a couple of hours rest I venture out again for food. A hamburger, accompanied by Pine Drop IPA, in some random bar and grill. Then it's time for bed.

The Flying Saucer
705 Main St
Houston, TX 77002
http://www.beerknurd.com/stores/houston/

Mini Book Series volume XXIV: Tour!

Houston Airport

Breakfast in my belly, I'm ready for the long ride to the airport.

As always, the motorway is like a roller coaster ride. I wonder that I've never banged my head on the roof.

Houston airport is an odd. Most airports are like shopping centres with a secondary transport function. Houston is eerily empty, with only occasional shopping and eating opportunities.

I need to pick up a present for Andrew. Some sort of history magazine. I have to walk a surprisingly long way to find a newsagent. All the way to another pier. But I do notice somewhere I can pick up a couple of sandwiches for the flight. They're so thick, they'll barely squeeze between my jaws.

That's most of my pre-flight activities done. Now I just need to fill up with fuel. Bourbon-flavoured fuel.

"A double Jack Daniels, straight up and an IPA."

"I can't serve you those together, I'm afraid."

"OK, I'll start with the IPA."

This is as bad fucking Norway, only letting you have one drink at a time.

I order some food to accompany my bourbons. Some chickeny thing. It's not the most inspiring meal I've had this trip. I pick at it with little enthusiasm.

Once there's enough bourbon warmth in my belly, I pootle over to the gate. It's going to be a long flight. AT least, for once, I don't have to work tomorrow.

Mini Book Series volume XXIV: Tour!

VI California

Mini Book Series volume XXIV: Tour!

Take California

Listening to the Propellerheads to get in the mood to write this.

Just back from my California trip. It was many things. Most of them fun, some a bit disappointing. But I met lots of old friends, talked endlessly about beer and other shit.

And met some dead cool new people, visited a new country, observed beards and tattoos, missed out on eating in Japantown and Chinatown in San Francisco, eat oysters in Baja California, bought my son Mezcal in Aladdin's cave, rode a commuter train, filled my camera's memory card in Toronado, drank a Heineken recipe brewed by Stone, had my first beer in a bar named Amsterdam, dodged breakfast (mostly), grazed on a barbecue doggy bag for days, photographed more buildings than people, snapped more kettles the faces, spent more on taxis than food, scribbled thoughts at the bar, paid more for orange juice than the accompanying breakfast, stayed in Victorian hotels, drank lots of cask, photographed pints in sexy poses, saw more trams, drank Californian Mild, watched fragments of random baseball games, an England team win a game, took enough photos to recall what the fuck I did, almost failed to find my own event.

Sat back and took a breath.

Mini Book Series volume XXIV: Tour!

Was reminded of the Berlin wall, rode in circles around Tijuana, drank in brewery made of containers overlooking the Pacific, tasted the mint in its garden, navigated by a roundabout Moctezuma, had my best meal in years, noted continued barrel fever, was bemused by pricing, remembered to pronounce it Plynee (and why it deserves the hype), learned to dodge San Francisco's slopes, drank Californian Mild in multiple pubs, walked a beach whose name I can't remember after midnight, grabbed surreptitious snaps in pubs, overheard someone describe taking his dad to a gay bar, learned of reverse commuting, spotted PCC cars in service, discussed the physical act of writing, gave most of my change to a sad looking man, forgot tram photos no longer excite the kids, saw street signs in Japanese, streets without street signs, pagodas, a drug free zone, cracked roads, brightly painted houses, stained glass banker's chique, the homeless piled desolately on pavements, ate tacos from a food cart. Appreciated Americana.

And drank some rather nice beer.

That's the highlights. Now I think about it, that's pretty much covered my trip. Magic. It'll save both me and you lots of pain.

Mini Book Series volume XXIV: Tour!

California!

Surprises. They can be pleasant. Like not stripping to my trollies and having my nads felt at Schiphol. Those Jamieson stiffeners before venturing to the gate weren't really necessary. I relativise, reflecting it is after nine. .... AM.

All I need for a long flight is a set of noise-cancelling headphones, free onboard booze, and an endless supply of mind-numbingly dumb comedy films. Films I'd be embarrassed to watch on TV, let alone buy a cinema ticket for.

KLM's selection is of crap films is crap. So I watch The Big Lebowski. Never seen it before. Unless you count the 30 minutes I watched in Czech, after a long session, in a hotel in České Budějovice. Largest hotel room I've stayed in. Almost as big as my flat. Understood it in the inverse ratio to how I'd lost it. The plot, I mean.

Back to the film. Reminds me of The Big Sleep. Which I guess was the intention. It whittles off a few shavings from the stick of time.

I need to stay awake. My body may be no temple, but it's my pad and I know where the

Mini Book Series volume XXIV: Tour!

woodworm and dry rot are. And get a cab.

It's my first time in San Francisco. Around the airport isn't pretty. But where is it?

Taxis are weird things in a strange city. You ask a stranger to drive you to location you've never been to before and you've no idea of the route. Like saying "Here, take my heart and my wallet" putting your life and finances in the hands of someone you know nothing about.

Every trip has its moments of paranoia.

My hotel keeps a fashionable distance from downtown. Like the elegant lady she is. I feel safe in a building that survived the earthquake (and fire). Plus it's not as arse-clenchingly expensive as many. There's a proper satellite box, HD TV, a fridge. And I can watch TV while in the shower.

Which I do next.

"Your schedule is crazy." Dolores told me.

Mini Book Series volume XXIV: Tour!

"I prefer to call it challenging."

I've an event this evening. Or club closing time as it is for me with the nine hour time difference. A train ride away. With a few hours before it to keep awake through.

The dust washed from my feet and the sweat from my armpits (and other places I won't mention) it's time to grab this city by the throat and say: "Can I have a beer, please? Sir."

Where to go? Has to be Amsterdam.

Soon I'll have my first beer on American soil in a couple of months.

Hotel Majestic
1500 Sutter St
San Francisco, 94109 CA
http://www.thehotelmajestic.com

Mini Book Series volume XXIV: Tour!

California! Amsterdam

Prepared is my middle, third and patrionymic when it comes to pubs. Knowing these hours between touchdown and eventing needed a non-lethal kicking, I came with something I'd made earlier.

I confess. A printed pub guide accompanies me on all my foreign ventures. Experience says: don't leave something as important as beer to chance. Noting the scarcity of licensed premises, I'm glad I didn't.

I'm on my way to Amsterdam, on foot. Amsterdam Café, that is. There's nothing symbolic about my choice. A pure arsing matter: it's the closest. And I've an impatient thirst.

I can just squeeze to the bar between all the empty stools. Is still quite early. Unless your body thinks it's early evening.

Mini Book Series volume XXIV: Tour!

The cheerful barmaid asks: "What would you like?"

Now there's a question to conjure with. I don't think "world peace" is the answer she's expecting.

"What's local?" I know. Fucking cliché. But I have to say it. My encyclopaedic knowledge ended when brewer numbers jumped from hundreds to thousands.

Evidently this is:

Headland Rye IPA

Not too murky, thankfully. Bit subdued, hop-wise. OK, but nowt special.

Cash only, I see. Bugger. Haven't great wads on me. Need to be careful with a couple of taxi rides coming.

Fuck. Look there in the fridge – there's

Mini Book Series volume XXIV: Tour!

[section redacted]

"Bedtime for Bonzo" my body is saying. "Only another 10 hours to go" my mind replies. Until I take a train to Palo Alto.

The barmaid gives me a couple of tasters before I choose my next beer.

"That tastes like an Irish Coffee. In a good way. But I'll take the Blond Stout."

Stone Master of Disguise
Weird. Pale, but with a coffee flavour. Odd in a way I'm still making my mind up about. Good odd? Bad odd? What the fuck. There's Spanish-language music pumping out, the sun is shining and the barmaid's bored enough to be up for a chat.

And I'm on my second beer. Always cause for celebration. Nothing lonelier than a single beer.

Only time for two. Time to take the Caltrain.

Mini Book Series volume XXIV: Tour!

Amsterdam Cafe
937 Geary St
San Francisco, CA 94109
United States
Open 12:00 pm – 12:00 am
http://amsterdamcafesf.com/

Mini Book Series volume XXIV: Tour!

Take the Caltrain

Redwood City. That's where I'm headed. I dive into a taxi, destination the Caltrain terminus on 4th Street.

My driver looks to be on the unfashionable side of 70. Though people keep telling me 70 is the new black. (I think that's what they say. I'm rarely paying much attention unless it's me doing the talking.) Seems he has a place in Nicaragua and lives there with his Nicaraguan girlfriend part of the year. Hope I'm still up to that at his age.

The station, as many in the US, looks ridiculously small for the size of the city. There are 10 platforms. But it is the main station for commuter trains heading south. Victoria Station it ain't.

A sarnie would be nice. But there's only a Subway.

It's a bit chaotic. Doesn't look like everything is quite running to plan. How quaint. There's a man hanging up a boards to indicate which train leaves from which platform. Or track, depending on your linguistic orientation.

Mini Book Series volume XXIV: Tour!

A bizarre white collar scrum forms, the middle classes battling politely for space. They know the train is going to be packed. I don't bother with any of that shit, but walk right to the far end of the train. In the commuting league, this Bradford Northern, not up your Arsenal. I get a seat. But soon it's jammed.

An accident has buggered up the schedule. My supposed express has turned into a Bummelzug. I'm already late for my lift.

I'm being met at Palo Alto station. I hope. By one of the blokes from the brewery where I'll be vainly trying to flog the rucksack full of books on my back. Late and I've no idea what my car date looks like. I wonder about a well-rounded bloke with a beard. Until someone confidently walks up and says "Hello, Ron. I'm Malcom."

He has a rather cool old BMW. In which he drives me to Freewheel Brewing. Site of whatever the hell it is I'm doing tonight. It's rarely 100% clear. I've learned to be ready for surprises. Like being told with five minutes' warning you're expected to talk on a subject, without hesitation, deviation or repetition. The hell version of Just a Minute.

A proud row of soldier pumps greets me at the bar.

"Pint of Bitter, please. Thanks very much."

Mini Book Series volume XXIV: Tour!

London Calling it's called. And full of casky goodness.

I don't want to get into any arguments. But when done right cask fucking knocks the spots off any other forms of dispense. Doesn't mean other methods can't deliver good beer. You just can't beat cask. But what do I know? I've only travelled the world searching out good beer for a few decades.

The lowkeyness of the event is probably for the best. And chatting about beer – now, you may be surprised to hear this - but I am quite keen on it. I'm getting a second wind. Is it the beer? The stimulating conversation? More likely that it's 6:30 AM in Amsterdam. When I get up.

Cask's caress against keg's spiked fist. Low carbonation is another reason to love cask. For me, at least. And, when we're really, really honest, we only give a fuck about ourselves. Mum, too, obviously. Maybe Dad, if he isn't a shit. And siblings. All close family, I guess.

I try several varieties of casky goodness, while my body asks: is it Wednesday or July? 10 PM is the answer.

A lift back to the city saves me more than the $7.50 train fare. A whole load of hassle. And the fear of falling asleep in an inappropriate place. I'm feeling that knacked.

Dwayne had a rare talent for falling asleep inappropriately. (Like on the train home. He always overshot.) And for being unwakeable. Not someone to take to a restaurant after a session. How often did we run off not without paying the bill, but without taking away our friend?

I sleep unsurprisingly well.

Tomorrow it's the infamous orange juice breakfast. One of the most traumatic experiences of my life.

Freewheel Brewing Company
Marsh Manor Shopping Center,
3736 Florence Street,
Redwood City, CA 94063.
http://freewheelbrewing.com/

Mini Book Series volume XXIV: Tour!

The infamous breakfast

I wake at 8. AM. Waking up is always a good start to the day.

I've only one thing on my mind: brekkie. The fried things on a plate with bacon kind. I need fuel for what threatens to be a long day.

I don't fancy eating in the hotel, but have spotted a diner on the map. Not too far away. And not up any hills. It's even on the same street as my hotel. The sun is shining and my appetite rising as I trundle down the hill.

Damn. They're shut. Don't open until 11:00. Pardon me? What's the point of a diner that doesn't open at breakfast time?

Time for some random hopeful wandering. What about the kitsch palace that's Tommy's Joynt? Maybe they do a fry up. It's not far. And not uphill, another important consideration.

It looks open. Staff are scurrying around inside.

"Are you open?"

"Yes, but just for drinks. We don't serve food until eleven."

I could hang around for a bit, a drink assuaging my hunger.

"Do you do breakfast?"

"No."

I'm tempted to say "Well do the trouser press, baby." But just turn and leave instead. Bum, bum, bum. Where to go now? There must be a breakfast somewhere nearby. Mustn't there?

Hang on. What's that over the road? Mel's Drive-in. Sounds like it could acquaint the spot with a damn good thrashing.

It certainly looks the part inside. Classic diner décor, even down to the staff uniforms.

You'd think after ordering as many breakfasts in the US as I have that I'd be confident of the fried egg terminology. But there's always a nagging doubt before I order: what's the order of the words "easy" and "over"? I could wimp out and ask for sunny side up, but that's not how I want my eggs. I go with "over easy" and get no weird look. Did I get it right or is tip anxiety at play?

Mini Book Series volume XXIV: Tour!

There's only one thing that can go walking out with breakfast eggs: bacon. But I have to think of my health, too. I order an orange juice.

Breakfast is decent. Though a slice of black pudding would have cheered it up. And me. You need iron.

I've a bit of a thirst thing going on. Because of the drought, you don't automatically get a glass of iced water any more. The orange juice was dead good, mind.

"Can I get another orange juice and the check?"

I go all American when I'm in the US. At least in a few terms. Nothing conscious. It just sort of happens.

The bill is a shock. $25. WTF? The food wasn't more than $10. Taking a closer look, I've paid $11 for two orange juices. That'll teach me to order without looking at the price on the menu. It was a nice breakfast which would have only been marginally less nice without the orange juice.

Lesson learned, older but wiser and several other clichés heavier, I climb the hill to my hotel. For a bit of a lie down, if I'm honest.

The sort of lying down watching crap TV that fills my time in hotel rooms. Occasionally spiced up with a dram of Laphroaig. Medicinal whisky – does anyone still prescribe that? I'd take them as my GP like a shot. And hopefully I'd have plenty of shots after I'd picked up my prescription.

Mini Book Series volume XXIV: Tour!

Discovering doctors had continued to prescribe whiskey during Prohibition was – how can I put this? – mildly surprising.

At three I'm doing a California Mild tasting at The Hog's Apothecary. In Oakland. It seems a waste to waste all the time until then. But there aren't that many beer places close by. My taxi bill is already demanding its own apartment. Don't want it growing any bigger. Once it sprouts facial hair, I'm done.

Time constraints rule out anything further than 20 minutes on foot. Unless I return to Amsterdam, that leaves one possibility. One that leaves me as equivocal as the backing singers on Equi's first album.

No time to grow facial hair. A temporary tattoo is the only solution.

Slider's Diner
1202 Sutter St,
San Francisco,
CA 94109.s
Tel: +1 415-885-3288

Tommy's Joynt
1101 Geary Blvd,
San Francisco, CA 94109.
http://www.tommysjoynt.com/

Mel's Drive-in
1050 Van Ness Ave,
San Francisco, CA 94109.
http://www.melsdrive-in.com/

Mini Book Series volume XXIV: Tour!

The dark side

Life's full of many things. Most brown, smelly and not what you'd want stuck to your shoes.

I'm not too bad with the jetlag thing. I can snap into new time zones with the same ease I can snap my ageing bones.

Yet something is very wrong. There's a pub. I've money and time. And I'm wondering whether I can be arsed to go there.

This is scary. "Do I really want to go to a pub? Do I need to?"

Pull yourself together, chav. Of course you don't *need* to go to a pub. You just fucking have to. Don't betray generations of pissheads because you're a bit knacked.

Dragging myself down the hill pub-wards, a familiar scent perfumes the air. Eau de I can't be arsed to find a toilet. "Students welcome" a sign says on a rusty hotel, prefixed by a particularly piss-perfumed pavement. Students of what I wonder. Urology?

Mini Book Series volume XXIV: Tour!

I've not mentioned where I'm headed, have I? Let me mention my excuses. Time. Place. Manner. (That is the right order, isn't it?) Don't judge me. No don't. Fuck off, will you? Fuck right off. I can drink where I want. Or, failing that, where I need to. (Time, place, manner: I've no time to drink anywhere else, it's the only place close enough, quickly.)

My destination is Mikkeller Bar.

For such a scrotum-stretchingly hip operation, they've shacked up at a surprisingly scrotum-scratchingly skaggy spot. Is that a good or a bad thing? Or just a thing?

Good, bad, exciting, annoying, fun, work. They're all just becoming things. Things I experience in those moments between eyelids up and eyelids down. And ultimately, between heartbeat on and heartbeat off.

Wait till you hit fifty. Mortality becomes less of an abstract noun. More of a stract one.

My belly and the bar embrace like the old friends they are. Beer menu? Yes, please.

Time to play hipster bingo. One point for every clean-shaven male, another for every female without a visible tattoo. Looks like the score is one. If I include myself. As hipster as you can get. Unless you can go less than zero.

Time for a beer.

Mini Book Series volume XXIV: Tour!

Bridge Road Little Bling 3,5% Session IPA
My god. A session IPA that's actually session strength! So why the heel is the serving 33cl? Quite dark but pretty clear. Hoppy and light. Not bad. Except for the price/serving size. $6 for 33 cl, while 50 cl of a 6.9% IPA costs $7. That's just crazy.

I'm feeling pretty wrecked. I had no energy at all when I got up. Don't feel much better now. And the walk back to my hotel is mostly uphill.

It's the usual trendy interior – minimalist exposed brick, chrome taps and wooden-topped bar. Oh look – exposed ducting. Hasn't that become old hat yet? I've always thought it looks crap.

I think I'm going to work my way up the IPA hill. A straight one next.

Tenderloin IPA 6.8% $7 (40 cl)
That's surprising. An IPA with no trace of murk Smells like lemon washing up liquid. But in a good way. I think. Very citrusy, which I guess is to be expected. OK. I could probably knock back a couple of pints if necessary.

Hope I've livened up by this evening. Sorry, later in the afternoon. I'm giving an informal chat on the history of Mild. Luckily it's a topic I can bang on about pretty easily.

The crowd here is about one third women. One or two blokes who look about my age, but most are under 40, a majority under 30. I feel like a Mass Observation scout noting down that sort of thing. Though I'll not be jotting down everyone's orders. That's way too complicated. There's a lot more on draught than Mild, Best Mild and Bitter.

Crux Half Hitch Mosaic Hopped Imperial IPA 9.5% $7 (25 cl)
Another clear one. I'm on a roll here. Oh, so that's what Mosaic tastes like: disinfectant spiced with mint. Not sure I like it that much. But Mosaic hops are hard to get hold of, so they must be good. Mustn't they?

A Swiss couple have just sat next to me. The woman asks the barkeep: "Which beers are on draught?" "All of them. This is the bottled list" he said, passing them another menu. Guess they aren't used to that many draught beers back home.

Just noticed they serve some beers at 40° F, some at 45° F and others at 55° F. Shit. Just noticed they have two cask beers. Fuck. I'm off after this one. Though I've not seen anyone order one so god knows what condition it's in.

I'm in luck. There's a cab waiting almost outside the door. Soon I'm rocking and rolling up the hill home.

Mini Book Series volume XXIV: Tour!

Mikkeller Bar
34 Mason St
San Francisco, CA 94102
http://www.mikkellerbar.com/

Mini Book Series volume XXIV: Tour!

California Mild

I've given up being surprised by life's odd twists and turns. Ride the rollercoaster and hope the brakes work.

Those beers at Mikkeller have, against all expectations, livened me up a bit. Or was it that Laphroaig stiffener in my room?

I've a long taxi ride ahead of me. All the way to Oakland. On the unfashionable side of the bay. Affordable side of the bay might be a better description. Those fucking yuppie bastards* are fucking up all the world's great cities.

A California Mild tasting is not so much down my street as off down the motorway, around the ring road, heading for Folkestone and the Chunnel. Talking about the history of Mild? My family haven't managed to stop me doing that yet. Despite making very clear statements about the fate of certain of my body parts should I persist.

It's an effing long bridge to Oakland. And a much less sexy one than the Golden Gate. I watch anxiously as the dollars tick up on the meter. I'd take a photo. If I weren't so hypnotised by the meter. And calculating how many of my rucksack of books I'll need to sell to afford the return fare.

What do I expect of Hog's Apothecary? Not sure. I could easily have perused the exterior on the internet. Now, why didn't I do that? Because you're a lazy arse, Ronald. Oh yes, I remember now.

Square box of a windowy thing, the pub. With a big open skylight. Look it up yourselves if you're so interested. I've Mild to drink, Mild to discuss and . . . Mild to tap? Er, no thanks . . . not while it's frothing crazily through the soft spile. Had a beer shower before. Way less fun than it sounds.

Mini Book Series volume XXIV: Tour!

Only two cask Dark Milds**, instead of the promised three. Still two more than I would have expected to find in California. And the missing Mild has an Ordinary Bitter substitute.

Today's talk is informal. Or me talking loudly about whatever comes into my head. Bit like an evening down the pub. Where I cling onto the talking stick all night. Maybe that's why I find it less scary than I should.

A year is a long time. In Brooklyn I was close to pebbledashing my trollies when given 5 minutes' warning of "an informal chat" of 30 minutes. Like much we fear, it's not that scary when you look it in the eyes.

Mini Book Series volume XXIV: Tour!

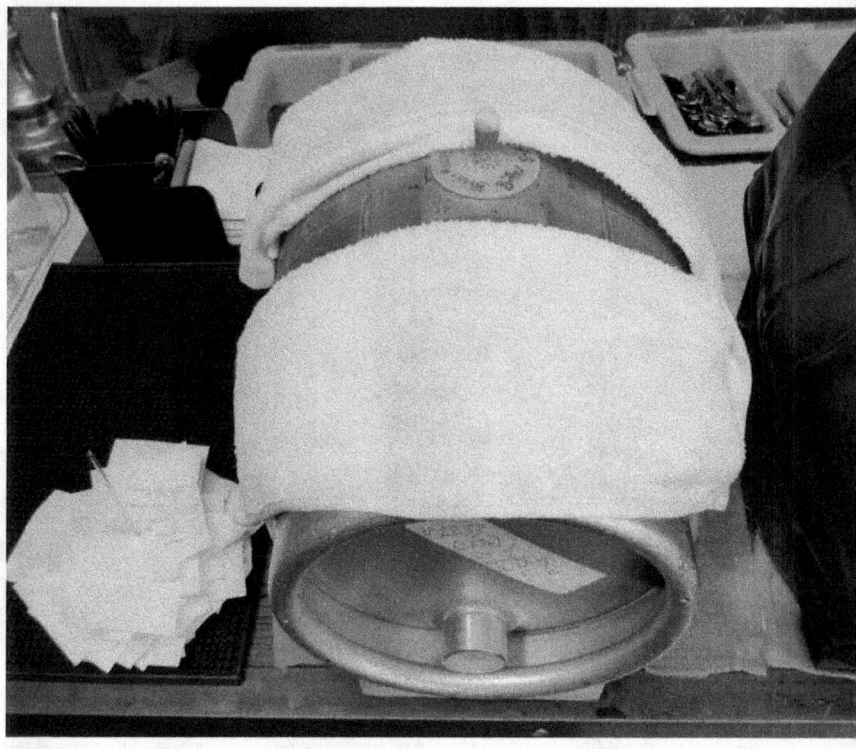

We're all a knotted skein of neuroses. Attracting the attention of the wait staff wracks me with angst. Chatting with a single stranger, too. But standing in front of 20, 50 or 100 strangers, talking beer, doesn't.

I linger a little, trying to flog some books. But when I'm offered a lift back to San Francisco, even the prospect of free beer can't hold me. My eyes are still watering from the taxi fare out here.

I don't go directly to my hotel. Instead getting dropped at my second porcine-themed pub of the day, Hogwash. I spot an old friend on the menu:

Mini Book Series volume XXIV: Tour!

Deschutes Fresh Squeezed IPA
The cask version of this in Portland left me an albino Dalmatian. One of my top beers of 2014. The keg version is full of juicy loveliness. But not as good as the cask. How could it be? One of the things I loved about it were its suicidal tendencies with regard to my throat.

I'm lucky to have got a seat. Probably the most unfashionable in the joint. But at least I'm seated. I forgot to eat at Hog's Apothecary. What's on the menu here? Nothing I feel like eating, sadly. Unusually for me, I just have the one, and head up Sutter Street in search of food.

At least finding my way back to my hotel will be easy. It's on the same street as Hogwash.

I get some food on the way back. In a Chinese restaurant. Hunan cuisine, it claims outside. I'm the only customer. It's 8 PM on Saturday. Not the greatest of signs. When I order a spicy dish, the waiter recommends something similar. An indication they've not quite everything that's on the menu.

Mini Book Series volume XXIV: Tour!

Falling asleep is even less of a problem than usual.

The Hog's Apothecary
375 40th St,
Oakland, CA 94609.
http://www.hogsapothecary.com/

Hogwash
582 Sutter St,
San Francisco, CA 94108.

Mini Book Series volume XXIV: Tour!

That's my country!

My joy at awaking every morning grows as the years are grated off my life's cheese. Why do I like grilled sandwiches so much?

Disillusioned by yesterday's breakfast fiasco, I choose the lazy option. And smash my fast with a huge hammer in the hotel. A bacon and egg hammer.

Posh, but near empty is the dining room. I check the menu. No nasty orange-shaped shocks today.

My charming waitress has an unnerving nametag: Nookie. Carry On films can't be big over here. It's only when the women's footie comes on in the bar that I understand.

"That's my country!" she tells the barman when she hears the anthem. Norway vs. Thailand is the match. I hope she isn't too disappointed by the result. Thailand gets thumped four nil.

The eggy bacony stuff I stuff in my stuffing hole is dead good stuff. What's on the dominoes today? Another expensive taxi ride.

Antsy doesn't do justice to my mood. I even had the location wrong until 5 minutes ago. It's not on hippy heaven Haight. But way out in the nobdocks. Taxi time.

American cities are a doddle to navigate. A simple grid pattern of numbered streets. I'm headed for 2505 3rd St. We pass 1st Street. 2nd. 3rd. 10th. 16th. Is it me, or are we going in totally the wrong direction? I'm tempted to say something. But I wouldn't say goo to a boose. Taxi paranoia is kicking in big time.

Overcoming my Englishness, I mention the strange streeting to my driver. Third is a mutant, twisting off 90 degrees from its brothers. Right. I think. But we do arrive on an improbable 3rd intersecting with 20th. Where I make my next mistake.

Spotting something called Dogpatch I tell the driver we've arrived. Mmmm... Something doesn't look right. The total lack of beer and a coffee theme suggest this might not be the right spot. Fuck. Where is it I'm heading again? I consult my trip document.

Bum. It has the wrong address. It has the Haight location. I've scribbled down an address. But it doesn't seem to be right.

Mini Book Series volume XXIV: Tour!

I wander off down the street, hoping to stumble across it. Most people would just look it up on their phone. But I don't have one that works in the US. I catch a group of young blokes coming out of a building. If they know where Magnolia is. They don't. But do have working phones. A few ticks later I'm much wiser. I need to walk another block.

Magnolia Smokestack is, as you could probably guess, a combination of brewery and BBQ place. I can see how that could work.

Owner Dave McLean hasn't arrived yet. I get a beer and my books out out back. In the brewery part of the building. As everywhere oak casks are stacked up against a wall. Oddly, most are from a distillery in Utah.

Dave arrives and we chat a little. It's pretty quiet. And the people out the front look more interested in smoked meat than beer history. But I've a pint of cask Mild in my hand. The sun is shining outside and there are free sausages. Things could be a lot worse.

Mini Book Series volume XXIV: Tour!

Eventually two people turn up. They're late because they'd first gone to the Haight Magnolia. I wonder if there is anyone still at the wrong location.

The event is so low key, it's subsonic. The worst turnout I can recall.

When Dave needs to leave, I hang around for some more cask and some BBQ. They give a month's worth of meat of various delicious kinds. I'd look pregnant if I ate that lot. Luckily, this is the US. There's a fridge in my hotel, too. I ask for a doggy bag.

Mini Book Series volume XXIV: Tour!

The waitress looks at my tray and says "Death by barbecue." She's not far wrong.

Had a pretty nice nerdy chat about beer, even if my rucksack is still as full of books as when I arrived. After several pints of cask Mild and Porter, I've now moved on to the IPA. Mmm . . . cask IPA. My favourite sort. IPA flavour without all the fucking burping.

Mini Book Series volume XXIV: Tour!

Proving Ground IPA
Pretty clear, a cask-style head. All that citrusy hop thing and low carbonation. Demonstrates why IPA works so well on cask. Hop flavour + drinkability. I had a couple of keg Imperial Stouts earlier. The cask IPA is definitely going down more easily. With less burping. Go cask!

It's getting dark by the time I ask them to call me a cab. I'm slightly disappointed no-one has answered: "OK, you're a cab."

It's a long wait. A very long wait. After 30 minutes - and the third PCC car - I get bored. I go back inside and ask them to ring the cab company again.

"Are you headed for the city? I'm just finishing, I can take you." A very friendly waitress says. That's another $35 saved.

It's too late to head anywhere else for a beer when I get back to my hotel. Instead a pick up a couple of bombers of Racer 5 in the nearest convenience store. That should keep me going until sleepytime time.

I've a free day tomorrow. One dedicated to fun, fun, fun. And dinner with an old friend.

Magnolia Smokestack
2505 3rd St,
San Francisco, CA 94107.
Tel:+1 415-864-7468
http://www.magnoliasmokestack.com/

Mini Book Series volume XXIV: Tour!

The Haight

No breakfast worries this morning. My doggy bag of BBQ contains more than enough for the rest of my stay in San Francisco. Possibly enough for the rest of the month.

With my taxi bill cosying up to Dolores and threatening to kick me out of my home, I decide to walk.

I should tell you where I'm going, I suppose. Or maybe why first. Or when. Or how.

Why? Because it's in walking distance (see previous comment about taxi bill). And I'm getting the hang of getting about in San Francisco: don't walk up a hill unless you have to.

When? Just before midday.

How? To the right. I've only ever turned left on leaving the Majestic so far.

I should have explored more. There's an offie much closer on turning right. And more.

Mini Book Series volume XXIV: Tour!

Japantown.

Whenever I travel, I have you're a fucking idiot Ronald moments. This is one. I could have eaten here rather in that spookily-empty Chinese.

I'm learning about the history of the city, as well as of my own stupidity. My hotel I know predates the earthquake and fire. Lots of the houses look Victorian. Then I find one with a date: 1878. Doesn't look like the fire troubled this hill.

Almost forgot. Where am I going? Hippy central.

Having read the Fabulous Furry Freak Brothers as a small child, and the classic "Needle Sharing on the Haight" as a sociology student, I couldn't drop in San Francisco without dropping by its old hippy heaven. And Toronado. A legendary boozer.

The sun is shining almost as much as the arse of my kecks. That's a bad thing. Not a huge fan of hot and sticky. Unless it's a barbecue sauce.

Drugs Free Zone? Confiscating pensioners' prescriptions are they? What total shite is that? You may as well declare an Air Free Zone or Dirt Free Zone. Ain't never going to happen.

Mini Book Series volume XXIV: Tour!

Despite the uphill section at the end, the walk is quite fun. In a sweaty really wishing I could afford a taxi sort of way.

Not sure what I expected of Haight Street. Fat Freddy, probably. He was always my favourite. The sort of chav to suck down suds with in a dive bar.

I'm surprised by how small an dive-bary Toronado is. That's a pleasant surprise. The barman, a sort of burned out old hippy, is convincingly surly in his service. I'm warming to this place already. This is my natural habitat, gut leaning on the bar, my mind freewheeling. Nothing to do but drink and watch and listen. I love pubs.

Now isn't that a coincidence? There are several Moonlight beers in their extensive cask list. The owner, Brian Hunt, is a friend. And a shit-hot brewer. Whom I'll be meeting later. I start with one of his classics:

Mini Book Series volume XXIV: Tour!

Moonlight Death and Taxes $4
Nearly black, tanish head. Just noticed they have two cask Moonlight beers. Damn. Oh well, I wanted to try this again, anyway. Slightly metallic, smoke coffee and toffee. Chocolate, too. This is nice. Fucking nice. Have a second pint nice.

Bum, bum, bum. I just filled my camera's memory card. And I can't work out how to delete images, old technophobe that I am.

God it's cheap in here. Even cheaper than the prices on the menu. Must be some sort of happy hour because there's a dollar off all the draughts. Cash only, mind you. Pay as you go. I do the leaving the change on the bar thing that I picked up when living in New York.

Time for another beer.

Moonlight Twist of Fate Bitter (cask) $4
Pretty dark for a Bitter. Just about in Dark Mild country. Fairly decent head and it's in reasonable condition. I was a bit worried about that. Biscuity malt, a pleasant undertone of bitterness, carbonation as soft as a wimp's handshake. Very drinkable.

Mini Book Series volume XXIV: Tour!

Moonlight Bombay by Boat (cask) $4
Much paler than the last beer. More hoppy, unsurprisingly, similar carbonation: soft as fresh puppy shit. Bit of citrus. Nice tasting bitterness again. Very nice. Again. Brian really can brew.

Mini Book Series volume XXIV: Tour!

Pliny the Elder $5
Very pale yellow, fuck all head. I can smell it from here. Has than lemon washing up liquid thing going on. That is nice. Loads of hop flavour. I can see why people go so crazy over it.

It's been a bit like a Brian tribute session – all his beers except Pliny. And that has a connection with him, too. It's what he brought over for me last time he visited Amsterdam.

The barman is pretty cool in a Big Lebowski sort of way. Just asked him if they have Guinness American Lager. They don't, so I've made do with another Pliny. That shows the power of advertising – I've seen TV ads for Guinness Lager.

I really like this place. The barman is starting to warm to me, even chatting a little. So different from the full-on trendiness of the Mikkeller Bar. And with much lower prices. 5$ for a US pint of Pliny – how reasonable is that?

I bravely return by foot. By a flatter route. I'm getting the hang of this San Francisco walking lark. In a boring, illogical European city, the streets would follow the contours of the land. And avoid unnecessary inclines.

Back in my room, I quickly unload images from camera card to flip flop. Want to do a bit of snapping tonight. I've a dinner date. With Brian Hunt. I couldn't visit the Bay Area without seeing him. A cool bloke and talented brewer. As today has proved.

The traffic has him running a bit late. I don't mind. The evening air is cool outside the hotel. And my mind can cartwheel with no obligations other than having a good time.

Brian is as bearded, opinionated and fun as ever. We bumble back Haight-wards in his van. This time the venue is *that* Magnolia.

Mini Book Series volume XXIV: Tour!

A very nice young lady gives us a tour of the brewery in the cellar. It's pretty cramped, as you'd expect.

Mini Book Series volume XXIV: Tour!

As I noticed yesterday, Magnolia is big on cask. Thinking about it, most of the places I've been to in the US in the last year or so have been. But perhaps that's self-selecting. Brewers of English-style cask Ales are more likely to get in touch with me.

We sink a few pints, eat and chat. Mostly the latter, as I'm trying to keep my belly from resembling a hippo's. And Brian has to drive home.

I pick up another couple of Racer 5s as a nightcap. To wash down my slumber-loosening Laphroaig. Sleep rushes towards me like a runaway train full of drunken soldiers.

Tomorrow I've an event with home brewers. Should be able to shift some books there, shouldn't I?

Toronado
547 Haight St
San Francisco, CA 94117
United States
Open 11:30 am – 2:00 am
http://www.toronado.com/

Magnolia Brewery
1398 Haight St,
San Francisco, CA 94117
http://www.magnoliapub.com/

Mini Book Series volume XXIV: Tour!

Freewheeling in Frisco

No need for breakfast angst today. Plenty of congealed barbecue in the fridge.

This is my last day in San Francisco. Tomorrow I'm off to San Diego for three nights. With a side order of Mexico. When did I last visit a new country? That's a good question. Almost three years ago when I went to Canada for the first time.

What's plan for the day? According to my itinerary document, I'm free until 6 PM. I just have to fill my time until then. If only I could think of something to do. I know – maybe I could drink beer in a bar. That would make a change.

My itinerary also has a list of beery pubs not too far from my hotel. Most I've either already visited or don't open until too late. Leaving a single candidate: Jasper's Corner Tap & Kitchen. Which supposedly has 18 draught beers. That'll do. I put on my walking shoes[8] and head East.

It's nicely overcast and not too hot. Lovely weather for a walk. Partly through what I call

---

[8] My only pair of shoes. Not just the only pair I have with me, but the only pair I own.

the Piss Quarter. Dodgy hotels with grand names and liquor stores line its streets. People sit on its pavements. I wouldn't, given the smell. I'm even tempted to hose down the soles of my shoes on return. A dazed girl with matchstick legs seems to be making a drug deal with two well scummy blokes. I love this city.

Jasper's isn't at all what I'd expected. Much more modern and upmarket. And rather bland. All the excitement of a 1960's airport bar. The dullest sort of modernity imaginable. As drab as John Major in monochrome.

I've no excuse. I could easily have checked on the internet. It's on the ground floor of a hotel. Rather swanky looking, in fact. Well, swanky in comparison to the piss palaces I've just passed.

Mini Book Series volume XXIV: Tour!

As usual, I park my fat sorry arse at the bar. It's pretty quiet, despite being midday. A solitary suited gent to my right, a middle-aged couple to my left. All drinking wine. Not a great sign. At least I don't have to look at the soulless seating from here. In front of me is a proud army of spirits.

The friendly young bearded barman (aren't they all nowadays?) tells me it's Taco Tuesday, they're tasty and cheap. Mr. suit to my right seems to agree. He's tucking enthusiastically into a row of three. "Maybe later," I tell him, "I need to work up an appetite first." I start on that straight away.

Mini Book Series volume XXIV: Tour!

Pine Street Atom Splitter $7
Ah yes! Here's the murk! Hazy copper. Not much aroma. A subdued citrus thing going on. Like music played several doors away. I guess it's a PA rather than an IPA (the internet confirms this). OK, but nowt special. What Do I care? I just want something wet and alcoholic to fill the afternoon.

Looking at the prices here, I realise Toronado is dead cheap. I could have gone there again today, but it's a bit of a walk. I'm getting a bit tight as I try to pay for everything with cash from my book sales. I only spent $30 yesterday and had two pints of Pliny!

There's a Golden Corral ad on the TV. It makes me want to vomit. Literally. Bad associations from last year. Best have another beer.

Mini Book Series volume XXIV: Tour!

Anchor Zymurgy Luxardo $8 6% ABV
Reasonably clear, very dark amber colour. Smells a bit like it's got Goldings in it. But ingredient guessing is a mug's game. Not so keen on this. Has a boiled sweet flavour and a weird caramel twang[9]. Luckily I've a side order of Buffalo Trace. That's really nice: sweet, spicy and with a touch of lemon. Dead good.

Last night with Brian was dead cool. We chatted away like crazy all night He's a great guy and brews brilliant beer. Odd how you can only meet someone a couple of times but become good friends.

---

[9] Actually it contains Maraschino cherries. Could explain the sweetness.

Mini Book Series volume XXIV: Tour!

Stone Enjoy By 9.4% ABV
Pale yellow, clear (once you wipe away the condensation). Yippee!. Smells absolutely fucking lovely. Every sort of citrus. That's what I call an American IPA[10] – juicy as a sexually aroused lemon.

I do believe my appetite has just walked through the door. It was worth waiting for him. I get a taco. $3 and pretty damn good. Especially with a good dousing of hot sauce. I'm tempted to get another.

I'm a lucky git. Getting to visit all sorts of places and meet all types of people. Even though this trip isn't working out exactly as planned, I'm having all kinds of legal (and morally acceptable) fun. Not travelling every other day is relaxing. I've had chance to look around and get to know San Francisco a little. Not that I've seen any of the sights. Other than Toronado and the Haight.

---

[10] According to Stone it's a Double IPA.

Mini Book Series volume XXIV: Tour!

Stone Enjoy By 9.4% ABV
Again. Say what you like about Stone, they brew some dead good beer. And I don't say that just because I'm meeting one of their brewers tomorrow. I hope. The whole San Diego thing has gone pretty much tits up. But, hey, failure is inevitable if you don't try.

I'm a bit buzzed. Unsurprisingly after those Double IPAs and bourbon. Time to walk home and have a bit of a lie down.

A bloke sat next to me at the bar in Toronado complimented me on still writing on paper. Is it really any different from writing on a computer? I'm not convinced. I think I write the same whatever the medium. Except with handwritten stuff I sometimes can't read it all. I guess I am more honest in my notes. Some stuff I'll never publish. Like . .

[*Redacted section*]

Luckily the walk back is pretty flat. Except for the last chunk of Sutter street. No getting around that. Next time I'll try to find a hotel that isn't on the top of a hill.

21st Amendment, the brewpub location of tonight's event, is downtown. I get a cab with

Mini Book Series volume XXIV: Tour!

what I think is plenty of time to spare. Except I have to cross the Financial District. And it's rush hour. We inch from one traffic light to the next. I've barely time to grab a beer before the fun starts.

I've been invited by Chris Cohen to speak to the San Francisco Homebrewers Guild. A, er, home brewers' club. About brewing historic beer. It seems I'm an expert on the topic. How did that happen?

The brewer talks a little before I'm on. He's miked up. Just as well because it's loud. We're in a small first floor section, while below in the main bar a raucous after work crowd roars and bellows, glasses clink and chairs rumble.

It's always a bit odd, these few minutes before I go on. Especially for unscripted chats like tonight's. What exactly am I going to say? "Hello, I'm Ron Pattinson, beer historian. Buy me a beer." Once I start, the words are always there, somehow. But there are always a few moments of doubt before.

How long do I speak for? 30 minutes? 45 minutes? I've no idea. I genuinely completely lose track of time. That's how much I enjoy listening to my own voice. Home brewers are a good audience because they ask good questions. OK, there's the occasional annoying

Mini Book Series volume XXIV: Tour!

smart arse, trying to show off how much he knows. Thankfully not tonight.

I shift a few books and chat beer when my talk is done. I don't stay too late. My flight tomorrow is at 10:15 AM. Meaning I'll need to be checked out by 8 AM. A couple of beers keep me company until it's time to put out my lights. Something that takes little effort. Especially after Mr. Laphroaig has paid his nightly visit.

Jasper's Corner Tap & Kitchen
401 Taylor St
San Francisco, CA 94102
United States
Open 6:30 am – 12:00 am
http://jasperscornertap.com/

"Brewer's Loft" at 21st Amendment brewery
563 2nd St,
San Francisco, CA 94107
http://21st-amendment.com/

The San Francisco Homebrewers Guild
http://www.sfhomebrewersguild.com/

Mini Book Series volume XXIV: Tour!

A busy day in San Diego

I finish the last of the barbecue before checking out. Jellied joy.

My taxi driver is thick, squat Russian, probably about my age. Which makes me feel much better about my own paunch. He talks on the phone the whole journey.

We pass several construction sites. New apartment blocks seemingly built from plywood. The word flimsy comes to mind. Not sure I'd want my book collection housed in something made of cardboard.

The area around the airport hasn't got any prettier since my arrival. I'm flying United and get dropped at their economy checkin. Only when approaching the checkin machine do I remember that I've got a first class ticket.

I've been given TSA pre again. Great. Shorter queue, less of a striptease required. I'd contemplated a fry up airside. But I'm not really that hungry. No rush to get to the gate, as I've a first class ticket. How on earth can I pass the time? Bourbon.

Bourbon is my greatest airport chum. Though nowadays there's often an IPA trailing behind him. Decent beer is getting pretty common in airport bars.

Did I mention that I've a first class ticket? It wasn't hugely more expensive than economy. Taking into account that I've two checked in bags which would have cost $25 a pop. And the dozen whiskies I plan necking during the flight. "Not really more expensive at all, Dolores."

The flight is packed. As pretty much every United flight I've taken recently has been. But the squalor is safely out of sight behind the first class curtain.

Surprisingly, I can remember San Diego airport from last year. Why surprisingly? Because I've been through so many airports, they've all blurred into one. The baggage reclaim is right by the exit. Just a few steps from the taxi rank.

Finding a hotel in San Diego was a nightmare. Most were either too expensive or too scummy. Finally I settled on the Britt Scripps Inn. It continues the historic theme of my San Francisco hotel, being a Victorian banker's villa. The staircase is gorgeous, carved wood illuminated by a leaded glass window.

Mini Book Series volume XXIV: Tour!

The house was built in 1887 and is furnished in period. Which makes the downstairs look like the set for an Edwardian costume drama. And that my room has a rolltop bath and no telephone. What would I do if I needed a wake-up call?

Mini Book Series volume XXIV: Tour!

I have to hurry. I've arranged to meet Kris Ketcham, brewer at Stone Liberty Station, at 4 PM. There are a couple of reasons why. He's a nice bloke. Plus he's recently brewed a recipe of mine and I'd like to try the beer.

I'd almost forgotten the humungousness of Liberty Station. And the oddly positioned the main entrance. The waitress seems to be expecting me and seats me at the bar. Soon a glass of Murder She Rotte is in my sweaty hand. It's a lovely shade of brown, as you'd expect from a Beiersch. It's a tasty drop. I'm pretty pleased. Pretty, pretty pleased.

Mini Book Series volume XXIV: Tour!

Kris turns up. His beard longer than ever. Longer even than those of Lexie's classmates. What is it with brewers and beards? I give him a bottle of Jopen Dark Gerste No. 1. It's the little brother of Kris's beer, Heineken's cheap and cheerful Dark Lager from before WW I. He puts it in an ice bucket so we can drink the two side by side.

Mini Book Series volume XXIV: Tour!

I have to admit a certain perverse glee in getting Stone to brew an old Heineken recipe. Kris doesn't seem to mind and is happy with the finished beer. We chat a little, but I can't linger long. At 18:30 I'm being picked up from my hotel.

When I'm in the taxi I realise that we forgot to open the Dark Gerste. Damn. I'd have like to have compared the two.

Sheldon Kaplan turns up on the dot. I met him last year on the sweltering afternoon a wild fire swept to within a couple of hundred metres of Stone's Escondido brewery. We've kept in touch since.

I've never been much far north of the city centre before. I'm surprised to discover that the original Spanish town was here, on the river, quite a distance from the current downtown. There's the odd adobe building, sometimes original. How did I manage to be totally unaware of this part of town?

I'm not quite sure what to expect or what's expected of me tonight. The original plan was for me to talk about Lager. I realise immediately that isn't doing to happen the taproom is inside the brewery and activity in the brewhouse is pretty loud. Looks like it will just be

Mini Book Series volume XXIV: Tour!

meeting people.

I spread a few books on a table and I await punters, beer in hand. Not just any beer. It's the final one in the set. Which set? Heineken Rotterdam's Dark Lagers from 1911. This one is the Bok and, if I'm honest, it's my favourite of the three.

People appear and chat with me. Amongst them Grant Fraley of ChuckAlek. Someone else I met on my last visit. He's driving me down to Mexico on Friday, something I'm dead excited about. It's not a huge crowd. A few books dribble away from the table. When that dribble runs dry, me and Sheldon take our leave.

He's promised to take me to Pacific beach. To, er, walk on the beach. Then take in a couple of beer destinations nearby. A long night gets even longer as we linger at length. In Amplified Aleworks a young woman sitting next to asks where we're from. She must have heard our accents. Mine, obviously, is English, Sheldon's a confusing mix of Aussie and South African.

Mini Book Series volume XXIV: Tour!

She's been stood up and decides to tag along on our drunken evening. We move on to another place nearby the TapRoom, which stays open later. We loiter until all the other losers leave. The latest I've been out by far this trip.

Sleep jumps on my back as soon as I undress. Without the help of Mr. Laphroaig.

Britt Scripps Inn
406 Maple Street
San Diego, 92103 CA
http://www.brittscripps-inn.com/

Stone Brewing World Bistro & Gardens - Liberty Station
2816 Historic Decatur Rd #116
San Diego, CA 92106
http://www.stonelibertystation.com/

Coronado Brewing Company Tasting Room
1205 Knoxville St
San Diego, CA 92110
http://coronadobrewingcompany.com/locations/tasting-room/

ChuckAlek Independent Brewers
2330 Main St, Suite C
Ramona, CA 92065
http://www.chuckalek.com/

Amplified Ale Works
Promenade at Pacific Beach Shopping Center
4150 Mission Blvd #208
San Diego, CA 92109
http://www.amplifiedales.com/

The TapRoom
1269 Garnet Ave
San Diego, CA 92109
http://www.sdtaproom.com

Mini Book Series volume XXIV: Tour!

Dossing with Diego

I'm not up to late nights any more. Cocoa at 9 PM is more my style now. I watch some crap TV while attempting to recover my humanity. It takes a while.

I've an appointment in the evening at Coronado again. But plenty of free hours before. What to do? If only there were some sort of place I could sit for a few hours, possibly with some kind of refreshment. I think I might recall just such a spot from last year. And not too far from where I am now.

One section of the way is disconcertingly steep. That'll be fun on the way back. I've chosen a hotel on a hilltop again – Banker's Hill in this case.

Last year my first evening in San Diego I spent on a session in Ballast Point. Seems a good plan to return. It has much going for it – lots of room, good range of beer (they had Dark Mild last time), decent food and most importantly of all, not too far away. Oh, and they have cask beer. Always a draw for me.

I slot myself between fellow barflies at the bar and peruse the tap list. Who am I kidding?

Mini Book Series volume XXIV: Tour!

I know where I'll start:

Dorado with watermelon (cask) 10% ABV, $5 for 8 oz.
"Could I get a pint, please?" I ask when I'm given a half-full glass. Only to be told a half is the maximum size they'll sell. Because of the strength. Probably a good idea, really. (I remember what happened after I insisted on drinking an Imperial pint of Storm King in New York.) It's a bit too strong for a full pint even for me, really. I can't believe I just wrote that. But it is only 12:30. I can't spot the watermelon. Not surprising, given the levels of hopping and booze. Pretty nice, but not something I could drink all afternoon.

Slightly disappointing event last night. What will happen tonight? Anything? I'm not optimistic. And I'm usually Mr. happy trousers. Good to see Grant and Sheldon. And to have a proper session afterwards. However hazy my recollections of it are. A beach, brewing kettles, a taxi home.

I'm so excited about Mexico tomorrow. Grant has set up a really cool itinerary.

Mini Book Series volume XXIV: Tour!

Black Marlin 6% ABV, $5 for 16 oz.
This fun. Just me and you (metaphorically), sitting at the bar. Nothing to do and nowhere to go. A Porter, black as a miner's kecks and beaded with condensation staring back from atop the bar. The sexy curves of the glass inviting an embrace. You cheeky temptress. I'm going to wait a while before succumbing to your seduction. Which I inevitably will. I'm only flesh and blood. First I smell your perfume, ashen as cinders. Then that first long kiss as you roll around my tongue. You naughty girl, you must smoke. Ok, this has gone far enough. Quite a pleasant Porter.

There's a real black-eyed beauty with her beau at the bar next to me. Buying a growler. Not sure why I'm telling you that. Other than it being a great opportunity for gratuitous alliteration.

The prices are very reasonable here: $5-7 for a US pint. It puts Amsterdam to shame.

The barmaid has just had a crafty drink, knocking back a quick couple of four ouncers. Can't say I blame her.

Mini Book Series volume XXIV: Tour!

Sculpin 7% ABV, $6 for 16 oz.
Pale and clear – no fucking murky sludge here. I'm going to have to keep some photos of San Diego IPA to show to twats when they try to tell me a beer should look like cream of chicken soup. That's really nice – very zesty. I think I'm starting to get this IPA thing. I've heard good things about this beer but don't believe I've drunk it before. Effing bitter, but effing nice, too.

I can't believe it. I'm cold. There's a real draught coming in through the door and I don't mean a pint of Tankard. I'm almost in Mexico, it's June and I'm feeling cold. Bloody global warming. The barmaid has put on a thicker top. Wish I had one with me. For some crazy reason I was expecting it to be warm.

I like the Sculpin so much, I get me another one.

Mini Book Series volume XXIV: Tour!

I've worked up a bit of an appetite. Time for a burger. The one I had here last year was pretty good. It's my first food of the day. Unless you count the liquid food I've been slurping down.

Mini Book Series volume XXIV: Tour!

Dorado (cask)
It's a bummer I can only get a half. But it is dead good. And 10%. Probably just as well they limit me.

I want to finish with something different. What about an IPA using an experimental hop?

IPA Experimental hop 06277 6.4% ABV, $7 for 16 oz.
Smells like tea. Not as good an aroma as the Sculpin. Mmm. Not sure I like this hop. Tea and earth come to mind. But not in a good way. This hop is never going to make it. Horrible flavour.

I just heard someone utter the immortal: "What's the lightest beer you have?" I'd serve them a glass of water.

My thing at Coronado is even quieter than yesterday. Only the chance to chat with Peter Symons saves it from total futility. That and the tacos from the food truck.

Mini Book Series volume XXIV: Tour!

Ballast Point Tasting Room & Kitchen Restaurant
2215 India St
San Diego, CA 92101.
http://www.ballastpoint.com

Mini Book Series volume XXIV: Tour!

Coronado Brewing Company Tasting Room
1205 Knoxville St
San Diego, CA 92110
http://coronadobrewingcompany.com/locations/tasting-room/

Mini Book Series volume XXIV: Tour!

Mexico

Grant is a little late. I've been hanging around on the porch for 20 minutes when he trundles up.

He comes bearing gifts. In beer form. The best form there is. There's a growler of Bohemian Summer Beer and a bottle of East India Porter. Both my recipes. Notice how many Lager recipes of mine have been popping up in San Diego. There's a reason for that. Which I may tell you one day. When the scars have healed.

It doesn't take long to get to the border. We're quickly through. A border guard checks our passports and looks in the boot. A dog comes a sniffing. Then we're in Mexico. Directly into the full-on intensity of Tijuana.

We take to the motorway which runs right up against the border. It's pretty eerie. The twin fences, no-man's land and proximity of a built up area conjures up an image from the past. The Berlin Wall. Except this one is to keep people out rather than keep them in.

We're headed south. To Ensenada where there are a couple of breweries where Grant knows the brewer. The landscape is much the same as the other side of the border. The buildings are very different. More random. Shacks and palaces intermingling like a cosmopolitan football crowd.

Part of the route is lined with shops selling ceramics a weird metal statues of dinosaurs. What exactly do you do with a 2-metre tall T. Rex? Is it meant for in- or outdoors? I'm weirdly tempted to buy one. Just as well it's 100% impractical.

Mini Book Series volume XXIV: Tour!

I've been to a lot of breweries in the last few years. In all sorts of buildings. But never one assembled from containers. As Aquamala is.

It's owned by a friendly couple, who show us around and feed us beer. It's a fairly small operation. In the taproom on the first floor there's a view of the Pacific and a cooling breeze. It's cool in both senses of the word. The garden leading to the sea supplies various ingredients for their beers. I'm impressed by their blackberries. Already ripe.

Mini Book Series volume XXIV: Tour!

Water can be a problem. They use the town supply and that's pretty erratic. Which is why they have a large tank filled with water. So they can still brew when the mains water is cut off. I can see brewing this side of the border brings extra challenges. Though water is likely to be a problem soon in California, too.

Next stop is Wendlandt, also in Ensenada. It's a bigger affair in more conventional business premises. The brewer shows us around and pours us beer from the conicals. It's pretty nice stuff. Even the one hopped with Mosaic. A hop I thought I didn't like.

"Why is the brewery called Wendlandt?" I ask Eugenio, the owner and brewer. It doesn't sound very Spanish. "It was my grandmother's surname." That's fair enough.

Mini Book Series volume XXIV: Tour!

Eugenio suggests we grab some lunch at a restaurant in the fish market, appropriately enough in the fishing harbour. A couple of his friends are drinking beer outside. The restaurant is popular. Too popular: we'll have to wait more than an hour for a table. So instead we go to Boules, a restaurant owned by another of his friends.

The people we met outside tag along. More friends and family turn up. Including Eugenio's wife and cute baby son. Eventually we're a party of nine, sitting in a garden restaurant. There's no menu crap. The waiters just bring out a series of dishes that we share. One of our party who own a vineyard pours wine from unlabelled bottles. Pretty nice stuff, deep red and powerful.

Mini Book Series volume XXIV: Tour!

The meal is a combination of meat and seafood. Crab, oysters, steak, lamb shank, wonderful sausages wrapped in vegetables and a flour tortilla and sauces. Three sauces: hot, hell and Hiroshima.

Mini Book Series volume XXIV: Tour!

That's the hot one.

It's one of the best meals I've eaten in years.

This isn't the Mexico you see on TV. It's a much calmer, more relaxed place. When I ask the population of Ensenada I'm told: "It's a small city. Just half a million people." Odd how the perception of town size varies. Someone in North Carolina was shocked when I called Newark, with a population of 35,000, a small town. She considered that pretty big.

On the way back to Tijuana, Grant suggests we stop at a grocery store he knows. It has a huge selection of tequila and mescal. It sounds like the perfect place to pick up a present for Andrew. The shop is bizarre. From the outside it just looks like a little grocery store. But hidden at the back there's another room. Crammed with every type of booze. Unsmacking my gob takes a while.

After much hesitation, I grab a bottle of mescal. It's not something you see much of in Amsterdam. I wonder about how I should pay for it, as I don't have enough pesos. Then I notice that the Mexicans in front of me pay with a combination of pesos and dollars. Seems to be perfectly normal. I do the same.

Mini Book Series volume XXIV: Tour!

We're going to drop by a couple of places in Tijuana. Grant has no satnav, but a brewer has drawn a simple little map. We just need to find a roundabout with a statue of Moctezuma. From there it should be a doddle. As long as we can find Hot Water Boulevard. A plan which, in a city that finds street signs optional, seems hugely optimistic.

Tijuana is a big city, with a population of well over a million. Amazingly, it works. We find Moctezuma and from there it's not too difficult. I can't believe it. Hours of hopeful, but ultimately futile, city circling was my expectation.

First off is beer bar BCB. Inside it's dark, upmarket and with a crowd of staff filling up the space behind the bar. The selection of beer – mostly US and Mexican, but with stuff from all over the world – is impressive. And not too pricey. I'm slightly surprised at Grant's choice of an Imperial Stout, given that he's driving.

We only stay for a couple before crossing the road to Verde y Crema, a rather nice restaurant. We sit at the bar and chat with the owner and barman. It has a decent beer selection, mostly fairly local Mexican stuff. I'm rather surprised to see Tennent's Scotch Ale in the fridge. I didn't realise they still brewed that.

Mini Book Series volume XXIV: Tour!

We don't eat much. Lunch was too large and too recent for that. But the nosh is again excellent. It seems Baja California has reinvented itself. Now American tourists, on the hunt for cheap booze, don't come in the same numbers, the region has concentrated on becoming a culinary destination. Better-off Mexicans from other parts of the country come here for its excellent food and wine. And beer. It's an eye-opener. Mexico is very different in real life to its image in the media.

Finding the border is a challenge. The signs indicating where it is seem designed to make you drive around in circles. We pass the same roundabouts several times before we finally make it. The queue is like an outdoor market, with people selling everything from hats to hammers. It's quite late and we don't need to wait long. Thankfully. I'm feeling

Mini Book Series volume XXIV: Tour!

pretty tired.

Tomorrow I fly back to San Francisco. But not until the evening, leaving me several hours to full somehow. What could I possibly do?

Cervecería Artesanal Aguamala
México 3
22760 Ensenada, B.C.
Mexico
http://aguamala.com.mx/?lang=en

Wendlandt Cerveceria
Boulevard Costero,
Carretera Federal 1 248,
Zona Centro,
22870 Ensenada, B.C.,
Mexico.
http://wendlandt.com.mx/

Boules
Moctezuma 623,
Ensenada 22800,
Mexico.

BCB Tasting Room
Orizaba 10335,
Neidhart, Centro,
22020 Tijuana, B.C.
Mexico.

Verde y Crema
Orizaba 3034
Col. Neidhart
Tijuana, B.C.
Mexico
http://verdeycrema.com/

Mini Book Series volume XXIV: Tour!

Farewell to Sandy Ego

Before checking out, I finish off the beer I won't be taking home with me.

Grant's Bohemian Sommerbier is the perfect breakfast drink: tasty, but not too overpowering. Sets me up nicely for the day.

Bags dumped at the hotel, I dawdle downhill downtown-wards. A couple of possible destinations in mind. Fortunately ones that open before lunch. Beer Co is my first choice.

Beer Company is my first choice. I don't quite make it all the way there. The Local tempts me in with its gypsy eyes. And a row of tap handles. I'm a fickle fucker. Time for introductions. "My gut - meet the bar." They embrace like old friends. Which I suppose they are.

Almost fucky-off time. Time to reflect. Let the good times roll, as Jimmie said.

Did I mention I once, several seeming lifetimes ago, I lived in the US? I must have bored you with that. "Shut up, dad. Yes, you lived in New York. Not interesting. Can I have 10

Mini Book Series volume XXIV: Tour!

euros?"

This is a weird as a weird stick platter doused in weird sauce. A thought so weird I'm going to have to lay it down on the pavement, walk away and consider it from a safe distance.

I can imagine living in the US again. I never thought I'd say that. Never going to happen. Family knots, work bondage, age. Age, that's the one. Too old for that crap.

Alpine Nelson (IPA) 7% ABV, $8
Hazy shit, man. Not quite sludge, but pretty thick. Mmm . . . Tastes better than it looks. Tropical fruit on the nose, very bitter at the back end. Better than the hue would suggest.

Looks very new, this place. Barn-like with loads of TVs. The toilets are very nice. Very clean. Though the pictures of muscly wrestlers on the walls are a bit disconcerting. I wonder what's on the walls of the ladies?

They seem part way through installing a brewery at the back. At least if the packing crates are anything to go by. Very handy for the tram here. The one line that they seem to

Mini Book Series volume XXIV: Tour!

have.

I didn't really plan coming here. I was walking by and in a fair need of a piss. I blame the growler of Sommerbier I drank before checking out of my hotel. A day of damp, stinky kecks or an unscheduled comfort break? No choice at all, really.

Mexico yesterday was super, super cool. Grant's a grand bloke and he introduced me to some great people. I can't remember when I last had a meal as good as lunch. Top, top nosh.

How's the trip been? The main event was a total fucking disaster. Especially considering how long it had been in the planning. On the other hand, I got to meet old friends, have some great chats, flog a few books, see Mexico and San Francisco. Overall positive, I'd say.

I should maybe eat soon. Not eaten yet today and it's 12:15. Though I did eat a load in Mexico yesterday. It's odd, now I think about it, that I didn't get the full fingerprint thing on the border coming back in.

Now I'm getting further down my pint it has some of the weird shit I didn't like in a Mosaic-hopped beer.

Just ordered a short rib burger. Meant to eat at the next stop, but hunger got the better of me. Or was it good sense?

Mini Book Series volume XXIV: Tour!

Mission El Conquistador Session IPA 4.8% ABV, $7
Not quite so murky, this one. Washing up liquid in the gob. Pretty bitter on the finish. And won't have me falling over too soon.

They have malt vinegar. Brilliant! Put some of that on my chips. Saturday in San Diego. My belly is full and I've a fair buzz on. And there's malt vinegar. Things could be so much worse.

Mini Book Series volume XXIV: Tour!

Hess Habitus Rye IPA 8% ABV, $8
Another pretty murky one. Citrussy nose, caramelly gob I wonder what the ears and hair will be like? This is a heavy beer. As pot-bellied as the glass What's the phrase? I couldn't drink six pints of it Quite a pleasant tangy orangey finish.

I'm surprised at how many cocktails they're serving. I suppose it is early afternoon.

I'm watching England play Mexico in the women's World Cup. Another punter is complaining about the lack of goal-mouth action. He has a point. But international football is all about tension, not action.

Mini Book Series volume XXIV: Tour!

BNS Revolver (IPA) 6.5% ABV, $8
Yippie! One that's clear. Almost. Can't be that trendy a beer, then. Pretty run of the mill IPA.

I'm chatting a bit with Jemma, the barmaid. She's married to an English bloke from Chester. And doing a pretty good job with the bartending, keeping everyone's glass nicely filled. I appreciate that sort of thing, impatient pisshead that I am.

The Bud anti-craft ad is on. Showing on a TV above a row of craft taps. Surreal.

I need to move on. The guy next to me just said "propane barbecue" and I first heard it as "cocaine barbecue". I suppose that's al fresco cooking for rock bands and film stars.

I stumble out into the sunshine and the short distance down the street to Beer Company. It's not all how I imagined it. It's a bit dark and old-fashioned looking. I'd expected something more like The Local.

Mini Book Series volume XXIV: Tour!

Elimination IPA 7% ABV, $6
This is suspiciously too clear. God I'm a contrary bastard. Moaning all day about my beer being too cloudy then complaining when I get a crystal clear one. Sparkling pale amber, no head. The aroma is pretty good, fruity-wise. Am I turning into an IPA drinker? OK, I suppose. Elimination IPA, I mean. Not me turning into an IPA drinker. That's definitely not OK.

Glad I spent most of the day in The Local. Nicer atmosphere, though the beer is a bit cheaper here.

Mini Book Series volume XXIV: Tour!

Broadway Brown 5.4% ABV, $6
Has the harsh roast taste all American dark beers seem to share. Why is that? Because they don't use sugar? I'd like me some sweetness in a Brown Ale.

I'm still feeling a little peckish so I order some onion rings. I won't be fed on my flight. I need to fill up now.

There are two types of traveller. The I'm going to turn up 5 minutes before I have to – just to prove I can – type. And me. Exercise is, generally, a good thing. A thrombie-threatening sprint to the gate, I'm not so sure about. Done it a few times. Rather stay on this side of premature death. That's why I get to San Diego airport with plenty of time to spare.

Enough for me to have a drink in the Stone Pub airside. An Enjoy By IPA. No need to get a bourbon, too. There will be whisky galore on the plane. I'm travelling first class again.

Stone Enjoy By IPA 9.4% ABV $7.70
Lovely fruity smell. Yum, yum. A really nice IPA. Wonder how much it's going to cost me? There are no prices on the menu. Oh yes there are. 11 bucks*? I should have looked

more closely. I suppose I'll make it last. I should do, really. I'm slightly wobbly. Could the mescal I had instead of breakfast be the reason? No, that's just silly talk.

It's getting quite late by the time I check into my hotel, almost 10 PM. I'm staying more centrally than before, but there don't seem to be a bunch of pub options nearby. There's Café de la Presse, which seems to be part of my hotel. But that's not very pub like. Not somewhere I want to drink at all. What to do?

I spot a liquor store up Bush Street. Where I invest in a small bottle of bourbon. Looks like I'll be partying in my room. Or something like that. It's a slightly anticlimactic end to my last evening in California.

* That was for 23 oz. (a size weirdly popular in airport bars). My 16 oz. serving was a reasonable $7.70.

The Local
1065 4th Ave
San Diego, CA 92101
United States
Open 11:00 am – 12:00 am
http://thelocalsandiego.com/

Beer Company
602 Broadway
San Diego, CA 92101
United States.

Stone Pub
Terminal 2, San Diego International Airport
San Diego.
http://www.stonebrewing.com/airport/

Mini Book Series volume XXIV: Tour!

Home

I check out of my hotel and get a cab directly to the airport. No time to do anything else. My flight is at 13:50.

As always, I've a plan. Noticed a food court airside when I flew to San Diego. Seems a good place to fill up on carbs before the flight.

Before I go through security, I remember something. That food court was in the domestic departure lounge, not the international one. When I see something similar landside I decide to eat there. No knowing what awaits airside.

I choose a trayful of dim sum. That should keep me going until Amsterdam.

There's a humungous queue for security. That's a bit of a bummer. The wait is seriously eating into my bourbon-drinking time. By the time I'm through, there's less than 30 minutes to boarding time. And I haven't found a bar yet.

According to the map, there are some possible bourbon-fuelling locations close to my gate. The first couple prove unsuitable, not having full bars. My last chance, right at the end of the pier is a pizza place. . . . with a proper bar. I sit at it. Giving my gut one last chance to be chummy with the furniture.

"A double Maker's Mark, straight up. And an IPA."

My IPA lasts four doubles. It's ticked around to boarding time and I really need to get going. Though I can afford to be one of the later boarders. I've very little hand baggage and an extra legroom seat. So not quite cattle truck class.

A couple of wines later I wander off to slumber town. For a few hours.

A taxi home and I've time to change clothes before heading off to work. It's going to be a difficult day.

Firewood Café
Terminal 3 Boarding Area F

Index

100/-, 146
19th century, 58
AK, 92, 178, 208
Ale, 11, 12, 18, 21, 44, 57, 85, 89, 92, 93, 107, 116, 129, 130, 146, 163, 178, 182, 184, 188, 206, 207, 208, 276, 291, 301
Amsterdam, 2, 4, 5, 7, 15, 51, 53, 74, 85, 127, 132, 137, 166, 168, 215, 222, 226, 227, 230, 233, 236, 257, 279, 290, 303
Augustiner, 99
Ballantine, 116
Barclay Perkins, 54, 114, 133, 146, 152, 163, 164, 178
barley, 114
Bass, 116, 188
BeerAdvocate, 133, 135
Best Mild, 178, 241
Bitter, 207, 208, 212, 232, 241, 244, 256
black malt, 218
Bohemian, 285, 294
bottom-fermenting, 114
British beer, 81
Brown Ale, 11, 12, 92, 107, 146, 178, 188, 206, 301
brown malt, 54, 73, 206, 211
Brown Stout, 59, 73
Burton, 116
Burton Ale, 116
Californian, 222, 223
CAMRA, 80, 81, 88, 95
Canada, 3, 50, 79, 80, 82, 97, 122, 159, 260
caramel, 116, 219, 264
cask, 11, 20, 67, 82, 93,

119, 123, 124, 133, 134, 138, 141, 142, 146, 157, 182, 184, 207, 222, 233, 241, 244, 246, 249, 250, 251, 252, 255, 256, 259, 277, 278, 282
České Budějovice, 224
Churchill, 150
CO2, 213
Courage, 152
Czech, 19, 224
Dark Mild, 49, 51, 80, 124, 162, 244, 256, 277
Double Stout, 73
Dry Stout, 66
Edwardian, 270
EI, 178
England, 116, 117, 189, 222, 298
Extra Stout, 142
France, 140, 143
Franconia, 203
Fuller, 101
Goldings, 44, 58, 207, 264
Grätzer, 44, 92, 172
Guinness, 81, 142, 194, 195, 257
Guinness Extra Stout, 142
Hell, 56
Hhd, 163
Hofbräuhaus, 53
Holes, 68
Holland, 2, 53, 144, 166, 200
homebrewer, 91
Homebrewers, 267, 268
homebrewing, 176
hops, 38, 55, 58, 93, 137, 156, 241
Imperial Stout, 66, 82,

195, 252, 291
India, 54, 58, 152, 283, 285
IPA, 16, 29, 34, 44, 48, 49, 54, 55, 57, 62, 68, 92, 104, 123, 137, 141, 150, 161, 172, 183, 187, 196, 212, 213, 217, 219, 220, 228, 240, 241, 246, 251, 252, 263, 265, 269, 280, 282, 295, 297, 298, 299, 300, 301, 303
Ireland, 156
Irish Stout, 73
Keeping, 51
keg, 11, 68, 101, 123, 124, 141, 182, 233, 246, 252
KKK, 146, 147
Kölsch, 55
Lager, 19, 34, 114, 194, 197, 257, 272, 273, 285
Leeds, 80, 196
Lichtenhainer, 44
London, 11, 54, 233
MA, 9, 46, 49
Maize, 208
Malt, 113
Matt, 162
Michael Jackson, 136
Midlands, 176
Mild, 4, 20, 49, 51, 80, 85, 92, 124, 138, 162, 163, 172, 178, 188, 196, 222, 223, 236, 240, 241, 243, 244, 249, 251, 256, 277
Mild Ale, 163
Mumme, 37
Munich, 53
Old Ale, 130, 182, 184

Mini Book Series volume XXIV: Tour!

PA, 26, 27, 31, 32, 107, 134, 195, 263
Pale Ale, 18, 129, 178, 208
police, 56, 60
Porter, 36, 52, 54, 58, 73, 101, 115, 137, 152, 163, 166, 178, 211, 212, 218, 251, 279, 285
Reid, 44, 57, 146
Running, 73
Running Porter, 73
Russian Stout, 95, 98, 164
S, 15, 27, 31, 126, 131, 179, 184, 185
Salzburg, 99
Scotch Ale, 129, 163, 291
Scotland, 34, 156

Sheepscar, 196
Sommerbier, 294, 296
SSS, 104
Stitch, 37
Stock Ale, 130
Stout, 34, 59, 66, 73, 82, 83, 95, 98, 100, 102, 128, 133, 142, 152, 164, 178, 195, 218, 229, 291
Strong Ale, 178
sugar, 37, 301
Tennent, 291
Tetley, 163, 196
treacle, 116
Triple Stout, 73
Truman, 146
TT, 146, 163
United States, 230, 259, 268, 302
USA, 5, 6, 45, 97, 106,

128, 145, 168
Vassar, 7
Victoria, 44, 231
Victorian, 15, 57, 82, 222, 254, 269
West Midlands, 176
Whitbread, 7, 12, 146, 163, 171, 178
WW I, 47, 272
X, 171
XP, 172, 192
XX, 133, 163
XXX, 146
XXXX, 44, 188
XXXXK, 92, 146
Yorkshire, 80
Young, 80
Younger, 104, 146, 163, 172, 178, 192

www.ingramcontent.com/pod-product-compliance
Lightning Source LLC
Chambersburg PA
CBHW071656160426
43195CB00012B/1485